Advent in Bethlehem

Reflections on Scripture and Bethlehem Today

— NICHOLAS TAYLOR —

Sacristy
Press

Sacristy Press
PO Box 612, Durham, DH1 9HT

www.sacristy.co.uk

First published in 2025 by Sacristy Press, Durham

Copyright © Nicholas Taylor 2025
The moral rights of the author have been asserted.

All rights reserved, no part of this publication may be reproduced or transmitted in any form or by any means, electronic, mechanical photocopying, documentary, film or in any other format without prior written permission of the publisher.

All quotations from Christian Scripture, unless otherwise indicated, are taken from the *New Revised Standard Version* (NRSV). © 1989 National Council of the Churches of Christ in the United States of America.

All quotations from the Qur'an are taken from the translation of M. A. S. Abdel Haleem, *The Qur'an* (New York: Oxford University Press, 2004). © 2004, 2005 M. A. S. Abdel Haleem.

Every reasonable effort has been made to trace the copyright holders of material reproduced in this book, but if any have been inadvertently overlooked the publisher would be glad to hear from them.

Sacristy Limited, registered in England
& Wales, number 7565667

British Library Cataloguing-in-Publication Data
A catalogue record for the book is available
from the British Library

ISBN 978-1-78959-401-0

Bethlehem University

&

Bethlehem Bible College

*beacons of Christian learning, witness,
and hope in a bleak world*

Contents

Foreword v
Preface. viii
Introduction. 1

Chapter 1. Rachel 15
Chapter 2. Ruth. 27
Chapter 3. David. 50
Chapter 4. Elijah 75
Chapter 5. Jesus. 101
Chapter 6. Epiphany Reflection. 132

Notes for Study Leaders 138
Further reading. 146

Foreword

The very name "Bethlehem" resonates profoundly within the Christian heart, especially as the days shorten and the season of Advent draws us towards the manger. It is a name synonymous with hope, with the dawning of light in darkness, and with the Nativity that forever changed the world. Yet how often do our reflections on Bethlehem remain confined to a cherished, perhaps romanticized, past? How deeply do we connect the "little town" of our carols with the vibrant, complex, and often suffering city of today?

In *Advent in Bethlehem: Reflections on Scripture and Bethlehem Today*, Nicholas Taylor offers us a precious gift: an invitation to a deeper, more challenging, and ultimately more enriching Advent journey. This is not merely a devotional; it is a work of profound theological reflection, historical sensitivity, and courageous engagement with the present. Taylor masterfully weaves together the rich tapestry of scriptural narratives associated with Bethlehem—from Rachel's sorrow to Ruth's faithfulness, David's anointing to Elijah's prophetic fire, and culminating in the birth of Jesus—with an unflinching gaze upon the contemporary realities faced by those who call Bethlehem home.

With the heart of a pastor and the keen eye of a scholar who has walked this land, Taylor guides us beyond the purely historical or the solely spiritual. He compels us to see the "House of Bread" not just as a sacred site of pilgrimage, but as a living community. We are led to consider how the ancient stories of dispossession, hope, struggle, and divine intervention echo with poignant relevance in the lives of Palestinians—Christians and Muslims alike—who navigate the daily realities of occupation, the shadow of the Separation Wall, and the constant quest for justice and peace. The poignant image of "Our Lady who brings down Walls" on the book's cover serves as a powerful emblem of this book's core message: that God's presence is found in the midst of pain, and our faith calls us to stand in solidarity with the suffering.

These reflections, born from ecumenical engagement and shared across diverse communities, challenge us to move beyond a privatised faith. They remind us that the Advent hope for Christ's coming is inextricably linked to our anticipation of God's justice and shalom/salaam/peace for all humanity. Taylor's work encourages us to listen to the "living stones" of Bethlehem, to learn from their resilience, their witness, and their enduring hope in a world that often seems bleak. He rightly points to institutions like Bethlehem University and Bethlehem Bible College as vital beacons in this landscape.

This volume is a timely and vital resource for individuals and groups seeking an Advent observance that is both biblically grounded and contemporaneously aware. It will undoubtedly stimulate profound discussion, heartfelt prayer, and a renewed commitment to embodying the peace and justice that the Christ-child came to bring. May these reflections open our eyes, stir our hearts, and empower our hands to participate in God's ongoing work of making all things new, beginning in Bethlehem, leading to Jerusalem, and extending to the ends of the earth.

++Hosam E. Naoum
Anglican Archbishop in Jerusalem
St George's Cathedral, Jerusalem

Preface

This book began as an Advent course offered across the ecumenical group of churches of which my congregation is a member. I would like to thank present and former clergy colleagues, and members of the Roman Catholic, Reformed (Church of Scotland), Anglican (Scottish Episcopal Church), and Independent Evangelical communities who participated in this. Some groups, drawn from different churches, met on church premises, others met in public spaces, including coffee shops and pubs, where their conversations over a proverbial pint could engage with those of neighbours and strangers celebrating Christmas prematurely. A subsequent iteration of the material was presented as an online Advent programme, enabling people in remoter areas of Scotland to participate in conversations, prayer and fellowship in ways that would be impractical in weather conditions at that time of year. My sincere thanks to all who shared in the recording, and who participated in these sessions. The material was also shared in groups affiliated with the Sabeel Palestinian Liberation Theology Centre in Jerusalem. I would like to thank

Omar Haramy for facilitating this, and for offering a wide range of suggestions for expanding and revising the text. I am grateful too to Archbishop Hosam Naoum for graciously agreeing to write a Foreword. Thanks too to Natalie Watson of Sacristy Press for so readily and enthusiastically accepting the end product, and seeing it through to publication. A grant from the Drummond Trust, 3 Pitt Terrace, Stirling, towards publication costs, is acknowledged with thanks.

I first became familiar with Bethlehem a quarter of a century ago, while Scholar in Residence at the Tantur Ecumenical Institute, located on Bethlehem land alongside the road that leads from Jerusalem to Hebron. Twenty-five years is a very brief period in the history of such an ancient city, but these years have seen enormous changes to the panoramic view of Bethlehem from the rooftop of the Tantur Library. Already in 2000, the city of Bethlehem and the neighbouring village of Beit Jala were swollen by the influx of refugees from other parts of the country, driven from their homes as the state of Israel was born in 1948. Many of these resided in the Aida camp, clearly visible across the valley from Tantur. Rachel's Tomb was also still clearly visible, and the ludicrous security arrangements which accompanied visitors to the site could be observed with some amusement. Since then, the eight-metre-high "Separation Wall", punctuated by the vast and forbidding complex of buildings and fences known as Checkpoint 300, has been erected, not only cutting off but cutting into Bethlehem, encircling Rachel's Tomb, and providing security for nobody. Israeli "settlements" have encroached upon the city on all sides, and on Beit Jala and Beit Sahour, occupying stolen land, consuming water profligately, and incrementally squeezing the life out of Bethlehem. And yet, in streets and churches once thronging with pilgrims, and in the homes of Christian families, the gospel of Christ continues to be proclaimed and to be lived in the place forever associated in Christian memory with his birth.

The birth of Jesus is not the only event in the biblical narrative located in Bethlehem, even if it is that which has shaped the city subsequently, both architecturally and in the Christian imagination. To appreciate the significance of the place at all adequately, we need both to take account of people and events of the Old Testament also associated with Bethlehem, and of Bethlehem today. The questions, challenges, and inspiration offered by those who live in Bethlehem today confront us. We need to seek through them God's word and God's will for us as we enter the season of the church year in which we anticipate not only our celebration of Christ's birth, but also God's judgement on humanity at the end of human history.

On the cover of this book is reproduced the icon of Our Lady who brings down Walls, written onto the Separation Wall in 2010 by Ian Knowles, founder of the Bethlehem Icon School. Inspired by the vision in Revelation 12, the Virgin Mary is depicted, pregnant and in pain, weeping for her children—not only Christ who was to die on the cross, but all who have suffered, and who suffer unjustly today. God is present in the midst of pain, and it is in the suffering of the people of Bethlehem and around the world today that we may discern God's call to us to make God present in the face of human misery.

View of Bethlehem across the Separation Wall, from the Tantur Ecumenical Institute. Photograph by the author, 2015

Introduction

The Gospels according to St Matthew and St Luke recount, each in its distinctive way, events surrounding the birth of Jesus. The Son of God is born to Mary, wife of Joseph, in the Judaean town of Bethlehem.

Bethlehem, identified as Bethlehem of Judaea in the Gospels, is located about six miles south of Jerusalem, in the highlands which separate the Mediterranean coastal plain from the Judaean desert and the Jordan valley. Another village called Bethlehem was located in Galilee, about six miles northwest of Nazareth. This Bethlehem is identified in Joshua 19:15 as one of the cities allocated to the tribe of Zebulun, and is almost certainly also the home of the judge Ibzan (Judges 12:8-10).

The name Bethlehem means "house of bread" in Hebrew, "house of food" in Aramaic, and "house of meat", or specifically of lamb, in Arabic. Bread is a staple food in many parts of the world, including the eastern Mediterranean region, and is sometimes used figuratively for all foods, not least in the Lord's Prayer (Matthew 6:11; Luke 11:3). A similarly idiomatic usage of meat is also found in Scripture (Psalm 145:15). There is therefore no significant change in meaning, from Hebrew to Aramaic, and even the transition to Arabic was less substantial in an age when most people ate meat only at festivals, and very few had any scruples about doing so.[1] What is of interest is that, with successive waves of imperialism bringing cultural changes to the Levant, the language of the people changed gradually from Hebrew to Aramaic during the Persian period (sixth to fifth century BC). During the Greek (fourth to first century BC) and Roman (first century BC to third century AD) periods, Greek came to be used alongside Aramaic, before the Arab conquests (sixth century AD) introduced Arabic, which has remained the language of the people ever since. While, as in other parts of the world, there have been population migrations, until the Zionist movement (late nineteenth to twentieth century AD), these did not substantially change the demography of the region. The Palestinian people are the descendants of the people who lived in the land throughout the long centuries of biblical history.

The earliest record we have of Bethlehem is found in a collection of nearly 400 clay tablets known as the Amarna Letters, discovered in Egypt towards the end

---

[1] In Daniel 1 we read of Judaean princes held captive at the Babylonian court who opted for a vegetarian diet. The principle at stake is not vegetarianism, but concern that meat prepared in the royal kitchens would not be *qosher*, i.e. would not necessarily come from an animal whose flesh was permitted under the dietary laws, and would not be prepared in conformity with the prescribed procedures which, *inter alia*, required that the blood be drained before the meat was cooked.

of the nineteenth century. The tablets, dating from the fourteenth century BC, contain correspondence between the Egyptian court and its military and diplomatic representatives in the Levant. The letters are written in Akkadian, a Semitic language, using cuneiform, a Mesopotamian script. In one of the letters, the vassal ruler of Jerusalem appeals to the Egyptian Pharoah for military assistance against a guerilla movement which had captured Bethlehem.[2] The town appears sporadically through the biblical narrative, most notably as the home of Jesse, visited by Samuel, last of the Judges, at a critical moment in Israel's history; the monarchy established under Saul had lost favour with God, who directed Samuel to Bethlehem, where he would anoint a son of Jesse to be the next king (1 Samuel 16). It is as the home of David's family that Bethlehem becomes associated by the prophet Micah (eighth century BC), and subsequent traditions, with hopes for the restoration of nation and kingdom under an heir of David, the Messiah:

---

[2] Contrary to the frequently repeated assertion of Nicholas Blincoe, *Bethlehem: Biography of a Town* (London: Nation Books, 2017), Bethlehem was clearly already a place of strategic significance at this early date. It does not follow that it was a major city in its own right, or even that the site was continuously occupied throughout the ensuing centuries. Ruth 4:1 implies a walled town, as does the story told in 2 Samuel 23:14-16 and 1 Chronicles 11:15-18. The account of Samuel's visit in 1 Samuel 16 suggests a recognized meeting place of community elders at the entrance to the settlement. 2 Chronicles 11:6, a much later text, records the fortification of Bethlehem by Rehoboam, son of Solomon, David's grandson.

> But you, O Bethlehem of Ephrathah, who are one of the little clans of Judah, from you shall come forth for me one who is to rule in Israel, whose origin is from of old, from ancient days. Therefore he shall give them up until the time when she who is in labour has brought forth; then the rest of his kindred shall return to the people of Israel. And he shall stand and feed his flock in the strength of the Lord, in the majesty of the name of the Lord his God. And they shall live secure, for now he shall be great to the ends of the earth; and he shall be the one of peace (Micah 5:2-5).

Bethlehem is located just six or seven miles (12 km) south of Jerusalem, the city in which David established his royal court and his son Solomon built the first temple. At the time of Jesus' birth, the whole of the Middle East was ruled by the Romans, whose vassal Herod reigned as king of the Jews. Herod was a bloodthirsty tyrant, as is known from contemporary sources[3] as well as from Gospel passages we will consider. Herod was known also for his building projects, designed to entrench and symbolize his and Roman power. One such project was the rebuilding and extension of the temple in

---

[3] The Jewish writer Joseph ben Matthias, more commonly known as Flavius Josephus, recounts several episodes in Herod's career in *The Jewish War*, book 1, and in *Antiquities of the Jews*, books 14-17. Amongst numerous others, Herod had two of his wives and three of his sons executed.

Jerusalem, the largest and one of the most famous religious buildings of its day. The same Herod also built the fortress of Herodion which towered over Bethlehem and the surrounding districts from a few miles away—a sight not unlike Mordor in the *Lord of the Rings* films.

During the time of Jesus, Bethlehem was a small agrarian town. That was to change in later centuries, when its significance as Jesus' birthplace made the town a centre of Christian pilgrimage and devotion, with ecclesiastical institutions arising alongside the agrarian community, and hospitality and crafts expanding the local economy and increasing the permanent population. More recently, the population of Bethlehem has been swollen as the city became a place of refuge for Palestinians driven from their homes and land during successive waves of Israeli occupation and expansion.

Bethlehem today consists of the "old city", rebuilt around the memories of Jesus' birth, largely through the influence and patronage of Helena, mother of the emperor Constantine, in the early fourth century. Jerome, a monk, priest and eminent biblical scholar, and his companion Paula settled in Bethlehem towards the end of the fourth century, establishing monastic foundations and pilgrim hostels for men and women.[4]

---

[4] One of the networks of caves beneath the Basilica of the Nativity has been identified by tradition as that in which Jerome worked. His statue dominates the cloister of the Latin (Roman Catholic) St Catherine's Church adjoining the basilica. The site of his monastery is unknown. Jerome was one of the first Latin-speaking Christians to study the Hebrew language, and to translate the Hebrew text of the Old

Wars and earthquakes have taken their toll on ancient buildings, but the Church of the Nativity remains essentially the structure erected in the sixth century. Monasteries, pilgrim hostels and churches, reflecting the diversity of ancient Christianity, surround the Church of the Nativity. More recently, schools, hospitals and other Christian institutions have developed within and beyond the old city.

The old city is surrounded by a modern city, which has expanded to accommodate not only its own natural growth, but also refugees who have lost their homes and land as Israel has expanded and encroached upon Palestinian towns, villages and farmland. This programme of ethnic cleansing has continued over the past century, and is the root cause of the continuing conflict between Israelis and Palestinians. Thousands of displaced people live in the Aida, D'heisheh, and Beit Jibrin refugee camps, others in tower blocks elsewhere in the increasingly confined space of Bethlehem, and in the neighbouring towns of Beit Jala and Beit Sahour.

Due to the influx of refugees, high-rise housing now covers most of the Shepherds' Fields, the traditional location of the appearance of the angels who announced the birth of Jesus to the shepherds (Luke 2), and the Fields of Boaz, identified by tradition as the farm of Boaz, the ancestor of King David, where he encountered

---

Testament into Latin. This translation, known as the Vulgate, was to be the standard biblical text of western Christianity for over a thousand years.

his future wife Ruth (Ruth 2–4), in Beit Sahour. Like many Palestinian towns and cities in Israel and the West Bank, Bethlehem is surrounded by "settlements". These fortified hilltop towns, and the agricultural land around them, have been seized by Israeli groups—without compensation, and without any moral right or legal title—from Palestinian farmers, many of whose families had tended that land for centuries. Very often, water sources are seized too, causing animals and crops to die, with consequent hunger, thirst and destitution in Palestinian communities.

Bethlehem is cut off from Jerusalem, and from much of its own agricultural land, by the "Separation Wall", the high concrete fence akin to those one might see surrounding a prison, which snakes through the West Bank, isolating towns and villages from the rest of Palestine, obstructing the access of many farmers to their land, and preventing freedom of movement between Israel and Palestine.

Most Palestinians, who do not hold permits (increasingly difficult to acquire) to enter Israel are forbidden to cross through the military checkpoints to work in or otherwise visit Jerusalem and Israel, or even to reach their own fields, orchards and olive groves if they lie beyond the wall. Foreign visitors may roam freely, and Jews from anywhere in the world can and do claim Israeli citizenship and seize land by force, destroy Palestinian homes, orchards and often ancient olive groves, and build exclusively Jewish settlements throughout Palestine. The brutality of the occupation today is a reminder of conditions when Christ was born, and the people were liable to have their land arbitrarily confiscated, to reward retired Roman soldiers and members and retainers of the Herodian family with agricultural estates, worked by dispossessed peasant farmers or by slaves.

For centuries, Bethlehem was a predominantly Christian city, with Latin (Roman Catholic), Greek Orthodox and Armenian Orthodox churches the most prominent. There have also been Coptic Orthodox and Syrian Orthodox communities for many centuries, and more recently Lutheran and other Protestant churches have been established. Monasteries, convents, schools, hospitals and churches serve the local community, as well as the pilgrim hostels and other facilities for visitors who have travelled to Bethlehem over the centuries. In recent years, Bethlehem University, a Roman Catholic foundation administered by the Brothers of the Christian Schools, has become a major centre of learning, as has the evangelical Bethlehem Bible College.

The influx of refugees from other parts of Palestine, and other pressures leading to emigration of Christians from Palestine, mean that most of the population of Bethlehem are now Muslims. For them the birth of Jesus is also a sacred event, and Mary (Maryam) and Jesus (Issa) feature prominently in the Qur'an. Places associated with the life of Jesus are therefore respected, sometimes even revered, and usually enjoyed some measure of protection during the centuries of Muslim rule over Palestine. It is not at all uncommon for Muslim families in Bethlehem, and elsewhere in Palestine, to keep a copy of the Bible in Arabic in their homes, to read it and to revere it as a holy book, alongside the Qur'an.

Bethlehem has been a centre of Christian pilgrimage since at least the fourth century. As we prepare to celebrate the events which our faith has traditionally located there, we need to remember that Bethlehem is not just a pilgrimage destination, it is also the home of people who live in poverty as they struggle to survive the social and economic consequences of the Israeli occupation, loss of homes, land, water and livelihood to Israeli settlers, from whom they are subject to constant violence and intimidation, as well as further threats to what remains of their land and water. In addition, many of the most educated and capable members of Bethlehem families have been and continue to be subject to arbitrary "administrative detention" by the Israeli security forces, i.e. imprisonment without trial for indefinite periods, or have been driven into exile.

It is right that we celebrate also Christ's birth, the Son of God coming into this world, becoming flesh and blood for us. The Church has always taught that Jesus' humanity matters: that he shared our physicality, and therefore our human needs, is essential to who he was—and to what God was doing in and through him. At one level, the place in which Jesus was born may be incidental, but we can also learn something through reflecting on the place in which the Gospels locate his birth.

At Christmas we celebrate the birth of him who became the bread of life (John 6:35), born to die for us (cf. John 12:24). Jesus gave his body, broken on the cross, for our salvation. At the Last Supper, his final meal with his disciples, Jesus took and blessed bread and wine, identified them with his body and his blood, and shared these with his disciples (Matthew 26:20-30; Mark 14:17-26; Luke 22:14-23; 1 Corinthians 11:23-25). Whenever we receive the body and blood of Christ in the Eucharist, we celebrate his death and resurrection, and our membership in his living body, the Church.

What does Bethlehem, a very particular "house of bread", have to teach us as we prepare to celebrate both our Lord's birth two thousand years ago, and our faith that, through him, God will bring to completion the salvation of the world made possible through Jesus' birth, ministry, death and resurrection?

In this series of studies, we reflect on how our faith connects us with the people of Bethlehem today. As we consider how God's work in that place over the centuries has formed our faith, how do we respond to God's grace in our lives, and also to the needs of those who keep the Christian faith alive in the place which bears unique testimony to the birth of our Saviour?

In order to appreciate the significance of the birth of Jesus in Bethlehem, we need to appreciate not only our own (western) Christian heritage, but also something of the diversity of often overlapping, sometimes competing, traditions which surround both the place and the people. Many of the stories we know from Scripture have been transmitted and cherished in Islam also; indeed, the two people mentioned most frequently in the Qur'an are Jesus and his mother, Mary. Even though these traditions have mutated somewhat, they remain recognizable, and the same is true also of David and of Abraham. Figures from Jewish and Christian Scripture are revered in Islam, and places associated with them are held sacred by Palestinian and other Muslims. Figures from the Hebrew Bible (the Christian Old Testament) are also significant in Judaism. While there has been much conflict between the faith communities over the centuries, this has had a great deal more to do with power politics than with religion. There has also been a long history of peaceful coexistence between people and communities of faith, and places associated with people revered by the different faith communities have been sites of shared communal festivities. However fragile that coexistence may appear in the present day, it is important that we appreciate it, and, as we come to celebrate the birth of the Prince of Peace, we consider what we may learn from the complex heritage of faith to which the Holy Land bears testimony.

We associate Bethlehem with the birth of Jesus, and with King David. But it is in the stories of two women that Bethlehem enters the biblical narrative. We therefore begin with Rachel and Ruth, before continuing to reflect on David, on Elijah, and finally on the birth of Jesus which we celebrate at Christmas. There are six studies, and it is envisaged that the final session, or last two sessions, take place after Christmas, about Epiphany time, so that the birth of Jesus and the events surrounding it may be reflected upon again, from the perspective of God in Christ being made known to the world.

Rachel's Tomb in 1845, following restoration and extension by Sir Moses and Lady (Judith) Montefiore in 1841, after damage in an earthquake in 1837. Engraving by unknown artist in Alexander Fletcher, The Devotional Family Bible: : containing the Old and New Testaments, with explanatory notes, practical observations, copious marginal references, &c. *(London: George Virtue, 1844 (?); New York: R. Martin & Co, 1845).*

The Separation Wall, cutting off Rachel's Tomb from Bethlehem, seen from the grounds of the Wi'am Palestinian Conflict Transformation Centre, photograph by the author, 2017.

1

Rachel

The first occurrence of a place called Bethlehem in the Bible is in Genesis 35. The patriarch Jacob has returned to Canaan from Mesopotamia, whence he had fled from his elder twin brother Esau (Genesis 27-28). The contest between the two brothers, as to which would succeed their father Isaac, as heir not only to his wealth but also to the promises God had made to their grandfather Abraham, involved extortion and deception on Jacob's part. The cost of his victory is his flight from the family home, to seek shelter with his maternal uncle Laban.

On his arrival in Mesopotamia, Jacob met Rachel at a well (Genesis 29), a recurring motif in the biblical tradition. Moses was similarly to meet his future wife at a well in Midian, and in very similar circumstances (Exodus 2:15-22). Earlier in the narrative, Abraham's servant met Rebekah, Jacob's future mother, at a well outside Haran, and negotiated her marriage to Isaac (Genesis 24). In the Gospels, we find this motif reflected in Jesus' encounter with the woman of Sychar, near

Samaria (John 4). In Eastern Orthodox iconography, the angel Gabriel meets Mary (Luke 1:26-38) at a well in Nazareth, and not in her home as in western Christian art. The well is a place of potentially quite significant encounter, and the first meeting of couples is resonant with expectation and tension.

When she meets Jacob, Rachel is tending the flock of her father Laban, bringing them to the well to be watered. Her name means a lamb or ewe. The story of Jacob working for Laban, the brother of his mother Rebekah, as bride price for Rachel, and of the mutual deception and intrigue that characterized his relationship with his father-in-law over a period of 20 years (Genesis 29-31), is less than edifying. After seven years, Laban gives his elder daughter Leah to Jacob in marriage, instead of Rachel. When Jacob confronts him over deception on the wedding night, Laban cites custom, and demands that Jacob work a further seven years to marry Rachel also. When his relationship with Laban is finally at breaking point, Jacob flees and returns to Canaan with his wives and children, and his flocks and herds. The journey is not without drama. They are pursued by Laban, claiming his household gods had been stolen—which they had been, by Rachel. Once having negotiated a settlement with Laban (Genesis 31),

Jacob faces the prospect of meeting his brother Esau. During the course of this encounter takes place also the mysterious episode of Jacob's nocturnal wrestling match, at the end of which he is given the name Israel (Genesis

32-33). Having negotiated his meeting with Esau, Jacob faces the prospect of war with the settled people of the land, after two of his sons precipitate a blood feud in revenge for the violation of their sister (Genesis 34).

After a sojourn in Bethel, Jacob and his family continue their journey southwards, heading towards the vicinity of Hebron where Jacob's father, Isaac, lived. Rachel, the mother of Joseph, is heavily pregnant with another child—who would be the only child of Jacob to be born in Canaan:

> Then they journeyed from Bethel; and when they were still some distance from Ephrath, Rachel was in childbirth, and she had a difficult labour. When she was in her difficult labour, the midwife said to her, "Do not be afraid; for now you will have another son." As her soul was departing (for she died), she named him Ben-oni; but his father called him Benjamin. So Rachel died, and she was buried on the way to Ephrath (that is, Bethlehem), and Jacob set up a pillar at her grave; it is the pillar of Rachel's tomb, which is there to this day. Israel journeyed on, and pitched his tent beyond the tower of Eder (Genesis 35:16-21).

Pregnancy is hazardous at any time, especially without the professional medical support taken for granted in the more prosperous parts of the world, but still inaccessible to many expectant mothers today. When constrained to travel during the later stages of pregnancy, the risks are particularly high. In the Gospel according to Luke, Joseph and Mary are compelled to travel from their home in Nazareth to Bethlehem, Joseph's ancestral town, late in Mary's pregnancy—and so Jesus is born in Bethlehem, the city of his ancestor David (Luke 2). Whereas Jesus was safely delivered, and Mary lived to see her son crucified and risen from the dead, Benjamin's mother died in giving him birth. Rachel did not live to see Joseph kidnapped by his brothers, cast into a well, sold into slavery and imprisoned, or emerge from captivity to rule Egypt and implement plans to avoid famine during a period of prolonged drought (Genesis 37–50).

In Islam, Rachel is remembered as the mother of Yusuf (Joseph), the subject of Sura 12 of the Qur'an. While Rachel is not named, both of Yusuf's parents migrate to Egypt, along with his brothers. They bow before Joseph, in fulfilment of the dream in which he saw the sun, moon, and 11 stars bow before him (Genesis 37:9-11; *Qur'an* 12, *Yusuf* 4):

> Later, when they presented themselves before Joseph, he drew his parents to him—he said, "Welcome to Egypt: you will all be safe here, God willing"—and took them up to [his] throne. They all bowed down before him and he said, "Father, this is the fulfilment of that dream I had long ago" (*Qur'an* 12, *Yusuf* 99-100).

Fulfilment of the dream required that Rachel still be living when, in his old age, Jacob migrated to Egypt. This is a notion which Islam may have inherited from the embellishment of biblical stories in Jewish folklore, as transmitted during the time of Muhammed in the Jewish communities of Arabia.

Rachel is not buried, as would have been expected, in the family tomb which Jacob's grandfather, Abraham, had bought at Hebron for the burial of Sarah. Abraham was himself laid there, as was his daughter-in-law, Rebekah. Jacob buried Rachel beside the road where she died (see also Genesis 48:7), implicitly somewhere to the north of Ephrath/Bethlehem. The narrative implies that the circumstances in which Jacob and his entourage travelled necessitated hasty funeral rites, rather than any judgement upon Rachel. In very much later rabbinic tradition, however, this episode is interpreted as signifying a contrast with Leah, who completed the journey to Isaac's home, and was in due course to be buried in Abraham and Sarah's tomb, alongside Isaac and Rebekah; it was in the cave at Machpelah beside Leah, not beside the road near Bethlehem with Rachel, that Jacob later wished to be buried (Genesis 49:29-32). Leah is understood to have been very much more the ideal wife of Jacob/Israel than Rachel. Not only did she bear more children, but she is remembered as having been faithful to the one God. In the account of Jacob and his family's flight from Laban, Rachel is reported as having stolen her father's "household gods"—cultic objects used for devotions in the home (Genesis 31); she is therefore, from the later perspective of rabbinic Judaism, implicated in idolatry. It was undoubtedly also significant that Leah was the mother of Judah, matriarch of the eponymous tribe, and ancestor of the royal house of David. The tribe of Judah remained faithful to the house of David, and worshipped in the temple in Jerusalem, while the tribes of Ephraim and Manasseh, the sons of Joseph, were to dominate the northern kingdom of Israel, and to worship at its shrines.

Rachel's tomb is identified by tradition with a site on the northern outskirts of Bethlehem, just 15 miles (24 km) from Hebron, and beside the road that today leads from Jerusalem to Hebron. It has been visited by Christian pilgrims to Bethlehem since at least the fourth century. The site later became a place of Muslim devotion also, and a square, domed structure was erected over the shrine. The tomb attracted women pilgrims in particular, especially those who, like Rachel, had been married for several years but seemed unable to bear children, and also those who feared the dangers of childbirth. The site was refurbished and expanded in 1841 by Sir Moses Montefiore, the president of the Board of Deputies for British Jews, whose wife was unable to have children. Montefiore was careful to preserve the Muslim character of the shrine, and it continued to be visited by Christians and Muslims as well as Jews, and especially by childless women. During the twentieth century, Rachel's Tomb became a symbol of Zionist aspirations, and since the Israeli occupation of the West Bank in 1967 has been administered by the Israeli Ministry of Religious Affairs. The precincts were fortified in 1995, and access restricted to Jews and to foreign tourists. Early in the twenty-first century, the "Separation Wall" was routed so as to cut off Rachel's Tomb from the surrounding areas of Bethlehem, and numerous Palestinian homes were destroyed in the process. Today the shrine and its approach roads are surrounded by high concrete walls with watchtowers, and can be entered only from the Israeli side of the Separation Wall.

To the north and west of Rachel's Tomb is Aida Refugee Camp, where several thousand Palestinian families who have lost their homes to Israeli expansion live in crowded and squalid conditions. Just to the south, and dominated by the Separation Wall, is Wi'am, the Palestinian Conflict Transformation Centre, an initiative of local Christians to support people and families traumatized by the Israeli occupation to find peaceful means to manage their circumstances, and to resolve the tensions within their communities which could otherwise lead to violence. Another near neighbour is Sumud House, a project of the Arab Educational Institute, a Pax Christi affiliate which works with women and young people in particular to promote peace and justice, and the coexistence of different religious and cultural groups, and to develop leadership and communication skills. They also arrange the annual Sumud Festival of Palestinian Culture. Also nearby is the Walled Off Hotel, founded by the graffiti artist Banksy, venue of the alternative nativity play produced by Danny Boyle. A little further away, near the Emmanuel Monastery, is the graffiti-icon of Our Lady who brings down Walls, written onto the Separation Wall. This image, inspired partly by the vision in Revelation 12, depicts the Virgin Mary, pregnant and herself in danger and in pain, offering maternal refuge, comfort and hope to those who suffer. The icon has become a place of prayer for peace and justice, that the Wall may come down.

Rachel enters the nativity story, briefly and indirectly, when the evangelist Matthew reflects upon the massacre of the children of Bethlehem:

> When Herod saw that he had been tricked by the wise men, he was infuriated, and he sent and killed all the children in and around Bethlehem who were two years old or under, according to the time that he had learned from the wise men.
>
> Then was fulfilled what had been spoken through the prophet Jeremiah:
>
> 'A voice was heard in Ramah,
>   wailing and loud lamentation,
> Rachel weeping for her children;
>   she refused to be consoled,
>   because they are no more' (Matthew 2:16-18).

And so Rachel is in a sense a type of Mary, mother of the afflicted, portrayed in the icon of Our Lady who brings down Walls. Her grief is reflected in the mourning of the families of Bethlehem, at the massacre of their children by Herod, and as they suffer recurring and often lethal violence today. Her tomb, once a place of solace and hope in the face of affliction, has been reduced to a nationalist shrine from which the people of Bethlehem are excluded.

Questions for discussion

1. There is some doubt in scholarship as to whether Ephrath/Bethlehem in this narrative refers to the same place as the Bethlehem known to Christian tradition. In 1 Samuel 10:2, Samuel refers to the tomb of Rachel in the area of Benjamin, which lay to the north rather than the south of Jerusalem. Jeremiah also suggests that the tomb of Rachel was in the vicinity of Ramah, Samuel's home in Benjamin (Jeremiah 31:15). There was also a Bethlehem in Galilee, northwest of Nazareth. The tradition locating Rachel's tomb on the northern outskirts of Bethlehem of Judaea dates from the early Christian centuries. Eusebius, Bishop of Caesarea and noted Church historian of the early fourth century, and his contemporary, the anonymous pilgrim from Bordeaux, both refer to the tomb at this site. Muslim and, later, Jewish traditions identifying the site are

dependent on these early Christian pilgrimage traditions. And yet, irrespective of the historicity, the site has been venerated, and been a place where women in particular have drawn comfort in times of distress. How important is it to you that "holy sites" be the actual location of the events with which they are associated?

2. In the biblical narrative, Rachel is the favourite wife of Jacob and the mother of Joseph and Benjamin, from whom the tribes of Ephraim, Manasseh and Benjamin descended. Yet her traditional resting place has attracted the devotions of Christians, Muslims and Jews, a place where women's hopes, fears and despair could be laid before God. Are women's experiences, in particular the suffering and danger associated with pregnancy and childbirth, able to unite people separated by religion, culture and politics?

3. Compare the fortified and exclusive Tomb of Rachel, as it has become, with the image of Rachel weeping for her children, and the icon of Our Lady who brings down Walls, with its symbolism of life and hope in the midst of suffering. Which of these images reflects our calling as a church, and why?

4. At the Basilica of the Annunciation in Nazareth, pictures of Mary from different parts of the world are displayed, in the church and on the walls of the surrounding compound. Each reflects something of the way in which Mary, the mother

of Jesus, has been received and become a symbol of Christian hope in a particular culture. How do you understand Mary in your context?

Points for prayer

1. Women unable to bear children, that they may know their human dignity to be undiminished; their husbands, that they may be loving, understanding and accepting.
2. Expectant mothers who face medical complications or other difficulties in childbirth, especially those for whom there are economic and physical barriers to receiving the care they need.
3. Women forced to travel during the later stages of pregnancy, in peril both of medical complications and of harassment.
4. The families of women who have died in childbirth, especially children who may feel guilt on account of their mothers' deaths.
5. The people of Bethlehem, especially parents who are helpless to relieve the suffering of their children.
6. The work of Wi'am, Sumud House, and all organizations which work to relieve human suffering.
7. Our churches and our families, that our Lord may be born anew in us this Christmas.

Naomi and Ruth *by Evelyn de Morgan. Public domain.*

2

Ruth

The first people of Bethlehem we encounter in the biblical narrative are the family of Elimelech and Naomi. Faced with famine (Ruth 1:1), they migrate to Moab, a kingdom to the east of the Dead Sea in the south of what is now the Hashemite kingdom of Jordan. Elimelech and Naomi, and their sons Mahlon and Chilion, are economic migrants. We are not told the cause of the famine, but drought, diseases afflicting animals and crops, and infestation of locusts were recurring threats to the precarious livelihood of agrarian communities in many parts of the world, including the Levant of this period. Elimelech, unable to sustain himself and his family from the produce of his land and animals, travels to a foreign country to seek the means to the survival of his family, presumably selling his labour, and that of his family, on the land or in the mines. It may be that the rigours of his labour, aggravated by chronic malnutrition, precipitated Elimelech's death, leaving

Naomi alone to raise their two sons in a foreign land (Ruth 1:3).

During their sojourn in Moab, Mahlon and Chilion marry local women, Orpah and Ruth (Ruth 1:4). We are told nothing about Orpah and Ruth, other than that they were Moabite. Later rabbinic tradition suggests they were sisters, while later Jewish folklore identifies Ruth as the daughter of Eglon, king of Moab. There is no suggestion of any royal connection in the biblical text. It is also intrinsically unlikely: kings' daughters were given in marriage to neighbouring royalty or to powerful courtiers, as a means of forming and strengthening alliances and ensuring allegiance. Economic migrants were not welcome or even tolerated suitors at any court, and their gaining the love of a princess, and overcoming the opposition of her parents and the competition from more privileged suitors, is the stuff of fairy tales. It is very much more likely that Orpah and Ruth would have been of the agrarian peasant community in which Elimelech and Naomi, and Mahlon and Chilion, eked out their living.

In due course, Mahlon and Chilion also die in Moab (Ruth 1:5), their lives quite probably also cut short by the conditions in which they lived and worked. Their names mean sickness and wasting, which could indicate the conditions into which they were born, as much as being attributed to them on account of the circumstances of their deaths. Naomi is left without any means of support, facing destitution and, quite possibly, homelessness. She accordingly resolves to return to Bethlehem (Ruth 1:6), trusting that, the famine having ended, kinship ties would enable her to secure shelter and sustenance in her old age.

Orpah and Ruth accompany Naomi on her journey from Moab to Bethlehem (Ruth 1:6-7). During the course of the journey—we are not told where, how far they had travelled, or how distant they were from their destination—Naomi releases her daughters-in-law from their obligations to her, and to Elimelech's family (Ruth 1:8-9). Orpah and Ruth are free to return to their country and to their families, to find there a security of which Naomi could not be assured when they reached Bethlehem. They would be at liberty to marry again, dispensed from the ties and obligations which had continued, in their widowhood, to bind them to their husbands' family. Orpah, after some hesitation, eventually gives in to Naomi's persistence, bids her a tearful farewell and returns to Moab (Ruth 1:10-14). She is not mentioned again anywhere in the Bible, but later legends embellish her story salaciously. She is attributed sexual promiscuity, and, in the Babylonian Talmud, identified as the mother of the Philistine soldier Goliath, whom the future king David killed with a slingshot (1 Samuel 17). Such an identification would be difficult to reconcile with the chronology of the period in which the story is set, as David lived three generations later. The Philistines, moreover, inhabited the coastal plain of the Levant, while Moab lay to the east of the Dead Sea.

Whereas Orpah returned to Moab, Ruth pledges to remain with Naomi, and to accompany her to Bethlehem, a stranger and foreigner to the home of her husband's family. In response to Naomi's persistent urging, Ruth makes the memorable declaration:

> Where you go, I will go; where you lodge, I will lodge; your people shall be my people, and your God my God. Where you die I will die, and there I will be buried (Ruth 1:16-17).

This implies a commitment not only to caring for her mother-in-law during her old age, but also to marrying a relative of her late husband's, so that her children could perpetuate his family. The explicit commitment to worshipping the God of Israel makes Ruth the first woman in Scripture to profess a new faith of her own volition. She renounces the deities of the Moabite pantheon, whom her family had presumably worshipped for generations. Moreover, Ruth's commitment extends beyond her life in this world, with her determination to be united with Naomi's family in death, as in life; the committal of her remains to their family tomb would unite her with this Judahite family for eternity: she would be "gathered to their ancestors" and "sleep with their forebears", to use the expressions with which death and funeral rites are frequently described in the Old Testament.

The story continues that Ruth participates in the barley harvest (Ruth 2), not as a paid worker, but as one of the poor and landless who follow the paid harvest workers, and hope to glean any grain they missed or dropped. This was the privilege of the poor, the means to survival for those who had neither land nor flocks and herds, nor specialist skills they could use to earn a living. Gleaning was not a handout, but gruelling labour which landowners were obliged to permit without hindrance (Leviticus 19:9-10). It was nonetheless not merely arduous work, but unprotected women were liable to harassment and molestation. Their story begins:

> And Ruth the Moabite said to Naomi, "Let me go to the field and glean among the ears of grain, behind someone in whose sight I may find favour." She said to her, "Go, my daughter." So she went. She came and gleaned in the field behind the reapers. As it happened, she came to the part of the field belonging to Boaz, who was of the family of Elimelech. Just then Boaz came from Bethlehem. He said to the reapers, "The Lord be with you." They answered, "The Lord bless you." Then Boaz said to his servant who was in charge of the reapers, "To whom does this young woman belong?" The servant who was in charge of the reapers answered, "She is the Moabite who came back with Naomi from the country of Moab. She said, 'Please let me

> glean and gather among the sheaves behind the reapers.' So she came, and she has been on her feet from early this morning until now, without resting even for a moment" (Ruth 2:2-7).

That the field belongs to a relative of her late husband's proves fortuitous for Ruth. Boaz is clearly a man of some wealth, having accumulated land which he was in a position to employ others to harvest. Her connection to Boaz, even though he did not at first recognize her, affords Ruth some measure of protection from harassment. The traditional site of the fields of Boaz is east of Beit Sahour, some two miles downhill from Bethlehem. If this is at all historical, then Ruth would, after a long, gruelling day's labour in the fields, have had to carry her gleanings (a considerable weight) uphill for two miles each evening. The work was exhausting, and there were the additional hazards of harassment, to which as an unprotected woman (i.e. with no father, husband, or adult son to defend her honour) and as a foreigner, Ruth might have been particularly vulnerable. The protection Boaz provides ensures that Ruth is able to harvest sufficient grain to feed herself and Naomi, and that she is able to do so without threat of molestation, but the work remained gruelling:

> Then Boaz said to Ruth, "Now listen, my daughter, do not go to glean in another field or leave this one, but keep close to my young

women. Keep your eyes on the field that is being reaped, and follow behind them. I have ordered the young men not to bother you. If you get thirsty, go to the vessels and drink from what the young men have drawn." Then she fell prostrate, with her face to the ground, and said to him, "Why have I found favour in your sight, that you should take notice of me, when I am a foreigner?" But Boaz answered her, "All that you have done for your mother-in-law since the death of your husband has been fully told me, and how you left your father and mother and your native land and came to a people that you did not know before. May the Lord reward you for your deeds, and may you have a full reward from the Lord, the God of Israel, under whose wings you have come for refuge!" Then she said, "May I continue to find favour in your sight, my lord, for you have comforted me and spoken kindly to your servant, even though I am not one of your servants" (Ruth 2:8-13).

That Ruth is a Moabite is key to understanding the story. In many passages in the Bible, foreign women are viewed as a temptation to Israelite men, through whom they would be lured not only into illicit sexual relations but also into idolatry (Exodus 34:11-16; Numbers 25:1-5; Deuteronomy 7:1-4). We have noted that Orpah's reputation is besmirched in later tradition with stories which defy historical plausibility, at least partly to exaggerate the contrast between her and Ruth, an evil, idolatrous, and licentious foreigner with the godly and virtuous proselyte (convert), whose acceptance into the nation of Israel the rabbis are concerned to justify.

The archetypal apostate, on account of his foreign wives, is King Solomon (1 Kings 11:1-13). Earlier in the biblical narrative, Abraham and Isaac take care to ensure that their sons, Isaac and Jacob, marry within their clan (Genesis 24:1-4; 28:1-5). During the period Israel traversed the Sinai peninsula after the exodus from Egypt, Phineas the priest slaughters Israelite men and their foreign wives, on this occasion Midianites and Moabites (Numbers 25:1-13). After the exile, the scribe Ezra requires that men divorce their foreign wives (Ezra 9:1-15; 10:44). The concern for religious purity, and faithfulness to the God of Israel, all too easily mutate into an obsession with racial purity, particularly when it comes to marriage and procreation.

There is a very deep prejudice against foreigners, and foreign women in particular, reflected in many parts of the Old Testament, but the book of Ruth stands in stark contrast to this. The book of Jonah is not so concerned with questions of sex or of religious and racial purity, but, like Ruth, it testifies to a recognition that God's providence extends beyond the boundaries of Israel, and embraces others whom Israel regards as enemies. Also of interest is the account of Moses' brother Aaron being reprimanded by God, and his sister Miriam being punished with leprosy, for claiming an equal prophetic authority to his, and speaking against his having taken a Cushite wife (Numbers 12:1-10). The struggle with racism, and appeal to religious sensibilities to justify it, is not new. It is a struggle we find reflected in Scripture, and which continues to beset human societies in the world today.

In the Old Testament narrative, the Moabites are almost invariably depicted as bitter enemies of Israel. Their origins are traced to the aftermath of the destruction of Sodom and Gomorrah (Genesis 19:30-38). When Abraham's nephew Lot and his family are fleeing Sodom, his wife dies—the narrative describes her as turning to a pillar of salt—and his daughters conspire to ensure that their family continues. They encourage their father to drink to excess, and while he is intoxicated, they seduce him in turn. The son born to the incestuous union of Lot and his elder daughter is named Moab, the mythical ancestor of the Moabites. This story reflects intense hostility and revulsion towards the Moabites, implying that the entire nation is contaminated on account of the sordid episode in which their ancestor Moab is conceived.

The exodus narrative includes the story of Balaam, described as a diviner or prophet who spoke the words of God. He is not of the nation of Israel, but is a somewhat mysterious and enigmatic figure hired by Balak, king of Moab, to curse the Israelites as they approach his land and pose a threat to his people and his power (Numbers

22-24). While Balaam refuses to speak words that God has not given him, and eventually pronounces blessings upon Israel, Balak's intention is to use Balaam, and the spiritual power he is perceived to wield, to bring harm upon Israel.

This is recalled by the prophet Micah, many centuries later, in calling the people to repentance, and to remember God's saving acts in the past:

> I brought you up from the land of Egypt, and redeemed you from the house of slavery; and I sent before you Moses, Aaron, and Miriam. O my people, remember now what King Balak of Moab devised, what Balaam son of Beor answered him, and what happened from Shittim to Gilgal, that you may know the saving acts of the Lord (Micah 6:4-5).

The enmity between the two nations reflected in this story is attested elsewhere in the Old Testament, in the story of the judge Ehud:

> The Israelites again did what was evil in the sight of the Lord; and the Lord strengthened King Eglon of Moab against Israel, because they had done what was evil in the sight of the Lord. In alliance with the Ammonites and the Amalekites, he went and defeated Israel; and they took possession of the city of palms. So

the Israelites served King Eglon of Moab for eighteen years. But when the Israelites cried out to the Lord, the Lord raised up for them a deliverer, Ehud son of Gera, the Benjaminite, a left-handed man. The Israelites sent tribute by him to King Eglon of Moab. Ehud made for himself a sword with two edges, a cubit in length; and he fastened it on his right thigh under his clothes. Then he presented the tribute to King Eglon of Moab. Now Eglon was a very fat man. When Ehud had finished presenting the tribute, he sent the people who carried the tribute on their way. But he himself turned back at the sculptured stones near Gilgal, and said, "I have a secret message for you, O king." So the king said, "Silence!" and all his attendants went out from his presence. Ehud came to him, while he was sitting alone in his cool roof-chamber, and said, "I have a message from God for you." So he rose from his seat. Then Ehud reached with his left hand, took the sword from his right thigh, and thrust it into Eglon's belly; the hilt also went in after the blade, and the fat closed over the blade, for he did not draw the sword out of his belly; and the dirt came out. Then Ehud went out into the vestibule, and closed the doors of the roof-chamber on him, and locked them. After he had gone, the servants came. When they saw that the doors of the roof-chamber were locked, they thought, "He must be relieving himself in the cool chamber." So they waited until they were embarrassed. When he still did not open the doors of the roof-chamber, they took the key and opened them. There was their lord lying dead on the floor. Ehud escaped while they delayed, and passed beyond the sculptured stones, and escaped to Seirah. When he arrived, he sounded the trumpet in the hill country of Ephraim; and the Israelites went down with him from the hill country, having him at their head. He said to them, "Follow after me; for the Lord has given your enemies the Moabites into your hand." So they went down after him, and seized the fords of the Jordan against the Moabites, and allowed no one to cross over. At that time they killed about ten thousand of the Moabites, all strong, able-bodied men; no one escaped. So Moab was subdued that day under the hand of Israel. And the land had rest for eighty years (Judges 3:12-30).

Wars between Moab and Israel and/or Judah are mentioned on several occasions in the Old Testament (2 Kings 3; 13:20; 24:2; 2 Chronicles 20:22). One of these wars is attested also in the Mesha Stele (now in the Louvre in Paris), a stone inscribed by the Moabite King Mesha to record and celebrate his victory over King Jehoram of Israel—a very different outcome to that related in 2 Kings 3, but which nonetheless testifies to conflict between the two kingdoms.[1] Moab is frequently condemned by the Prophets for oppression and violence (Isaiah 25:10; Jeremiah 48; Ezekiel 25:8-11; Amos 2:1-3; Zephaniah 2:8-11), but there is also grief at its destruction:

> My heart cries out for Moab; his fugitives flee to Zoar, to Eglath-shelishiyah. For at the ascent of Luhith they go up weeping; on the road to Horonaim they raise a cry of destruction; the waters of Nimrim are a desolation; the grass is withered, the new growth fails, the verdure is no more (Isaiah 15:5-6).

Moabite women are described as having seduced Israelite men, and caused them to apostatize from the exclusive worship of their God, and to participate in pagan cults:

> While Israel was staying at Shittim, the people began to have sexual relations with the women of Moab. These invited the people to the sacrifices of their gods, and the people ate and bowed down to their gods. Thus Israel yoked

---

[1] It is not surprising that in both the biblical account and the Stele the authors claim victory for their own nation and king. While the precise course of events is impossible to reconstruct, most scholars tend to favour the Mesha Stele as the more contemporary record.

itself to the Baal of Peor, and the Lord's anger was kindled against Israel. The Lord said to Moses, "Take all the chiefs of the people, and impale them in the sun before the Lord, in order that the fierce anger of the Lord may turn away from Israel." And Moses said to the judges of Israel, "Each of you shall kill any of your people who have yoked themselves to the Baal of Peor" (Numbers 25:1-5).

The well-known trope of women being to blame for the sexual and other actions of men is attested even in Scripture. There are overtones of this in the story of Ruth, when, at Naomi's instigation, she attends the festivities which accompany the threshing of the harvest:

So she went down to the threshing-floor and did just as her mother-in-law had instructed her. When Boaz had eaten and drunk, and he was in a contented mood, he went to lie down at the end of the heap of grain. Then she came quietly and uncovered his feet, and lay down. At midnight the man was startled and turned over, and there, lying at his feet, was a woman! He said, "Who are you?" And she answered, "I am Ruth, your servant; spread your cloak over your servant, for you are next-of-kin." He said, "May you be blessed by the Lord, my daughter; this last instance of your loyalty is better than the first; you have not gone after young men, whether poor or rich. And now, my daughter, do not be afraid; I will do for you all that you ask, for all the assembly of my people know that you are a worthy woman. But now, though it is true that I am a near kinsman, there is another kinsman more closely related than I. Remain this night, and in the morning, if he will act as next-of-kin for you, good; let him do so. If he is not willing to act as next-of-kin for you, then, as the Lord lives, I will act as next-of-kin for you. Lie down until the morning" (Ruth 3:6-13).

At the very least, Ruth gives Boaz reason to believe that she had seduced and entrapped him while he was drunk. The expression "uncovered his feet" may be euphemistic for the genitals. She certainly seeks his attention at an occasion on which fertility was celebrated, and at which normal inhibitions might be affected by alcohol. However, in following Naomi's instructions, Ruth is seeking to fulfil her duty to the family into which she had married. Marriage to Boaz would enable a close relation of her late husband to father a child whom she would raise to be heir to Elimelech and Mahlon, continue their family, and tend their land.

Boaz initially defers to a relation who stood closer to Elimelech and Mahlon than he did, but when the unnamed relative declines to marry Ruth, Boaz proceeds to do so (Ruth 4:1-12). The negotiations at the town gate, the customary place of meeting, are concerned as much about property as they are about marriage and procreation. Indeed, the anonymous relative is willing to acquire the land which had formerly belonged to Elimelech, but only to extend his own estate; he is unwilling to marry Ruth and see a child of that marriage inherit the land which he wished to acquire (Ruth 4:6). This frees Boaz to redeem Elimelech's property and to marry Ruth, which he proceeds to do. Their child, Obed, is deemed to be the son of Mahlon, and thus a grandchild to Naomi (Ruth 4:13-17). Obed is identified as the father of Jesse, the father of David (Ruth 4:21-22), who was to become king and founder of the dynasty which ruled from Jerusalem for several centuries.

The concerns with sexual propriety, particularly on the part of women, apparent in the book of Ruth, and in other parts of the Old Testament, are reflected also in the nativity story in the Gospel of Matthew. Joseph's immediate response to learning that Mary was pregnant before their marriage, was to assume that she had done something shameful, and to withdraw from their betrothal:

> [Mary's] husband Joseph, being a righteous man and unwilling to expose her to public disgrace, planned to dismiss her quietly. But just when he had resolved to do this, an angel of the Lord appeared to him in a dream and said, "Joseph, son of David, do not be afraid to

take Mary as your wife, for the child conceived in her is from the Holy Spirit. She will bear a son, and you are to name him Jesus, for he will save his people from their sins." All this took place to fulfil what had been spoken by the Lord through the prophet:

"Look, the virgin shall conceive and bear a son, and they shall name him Emmanuel", which means, "God is with us." When Joseph awoke from sleep, he did as the angel of the Lord commanded him; he took her as his wife, but had no marital relations with her until she had borne a son; and he named him Jesus (Matthew 1:19-25).

It is only after he has received from the angel assurances of Mary's virtue and of God's purpose in her pregnancy, that Joseph proceeds with the marriage.

The book of Ruth testifies to a very different ethos to that which we find in many other books of the Old Testament. There is no hint of the particularism—ethnic and religious exclusivity—which characterizes many of the laws which regulate Israel's relations with people of other nations. There is no suggestion that Ruth is ethnically impure, or condemned for her earlier worship of the gods of Moab. On the contrary, her faithfulness and care for Naomi merits respect, and she is considered a worthy matriarch of the royal dynasty: the child she bears for Mahlon, through her marriage to Boaz, is identified as the paternal grandfather of King David.

In the Gospel of Matthew, Ruth is identified as an ancestor of Jesus (Matthew 1:5). She is one of five women named in an otherwise all-male genealogy; the others being Tamar (Matthew 1:3), the daughter-in-law of Judah, son of Jacob, whom she lured into an illicit liaison (Genesis 38:12-23); Rahab, the Canaanite prostitute of Jericho (Joshua 2), identified as the mother of Boaz (Matthew 1:5);[2] Bathsheba (Matthew 1:6), the wife of Uriah the Hittite, whose death in battle David arranged in order to cover up and then regularize his adultery—and, quite probably, abuse of power—before she gave birth to Solomon, and with the prophet Nathan orchestrated his succession to David's throne (2 Samuel 11-12; 1 Kings 1:15-31); and Mary, wife of Joseph and mother of Jesus (Matthew 1:16). Scholars have been intrigued by the naming of these women, and how they are connected to Mary, the mother of Jesus. Rahab, Ruth, and by implication Tamar, are born outside the nation of Israel and incorporated through marriage, while Bathsheba was married to a foreigner, a Hittite mercenary in David's army, before marrying David. Irregular sexual behaviour features in the stories of Tamar, Rahab, Bathsheba and, possibly, Ruth. And

---

[2] Rahab's identity and profession are subject to speculation in later Jewish and Christian tradition and folklore. Elsewhere in the New Testament she is described as a person of faith (Hebrews 11:31) and of good works (James 2:25), despite her profession before the fall of Jericho.

yet they are ancestors of the royal line of David, and accordingly have their place in the genealogy of Jesus; a place which the evangelist Matthew emphasizes, and connects with the role of Mary, the mother of Jesus.

The story of Ruth can enrich our Advent reflections in many ways. Ancient prejudices overcome challenge us, as we prepare for God's judgement upon us, to be conscious of prejudice, exploitation and persecution in the world today. Issues of race and gender continue to shape cultures, and discrimination—especially against migrants—is defended on grounds of culture. In Ruth we find an example, perhaps apparently insignificant in itself, in which barriers to human flourishing are transcended, and God's providence is seen to embrace those considered outsiders. The birth of Jesus is an event in continuity with, and made possible by, Ruth's life. Ruth, in her way, points to the new humanity in Christ's body (Ephesians 2:15-16), in which we are all called to share, and for which we are all called to work.

Questions for discussion

1. The Mesha Stele and the biblical account of the war between Moab and Israel in 2 Kings 3 are, as historical records of the same event, irreconcilable. How important is it that events related in the Bible took place precisely as recounted?

2. The Moabites are typically depicted in the Old Testament as intrinsically evil, hostile to God and to God's people, idolaters to be avoided in all circumstances. Yet Elimelech and his family were able to live as refugees in Moab, and to find a means of livelihood there, as do many Palestinians who have fled to Jordan in recent decades. Not only were they tolerated as what we might call "economic migrants", but Mahlon and Chilion were able to marry Moabite women. What kind of welcome would you hope for if circumstances constrained you to seek refuge in a strange land, whose people you don't know, and against whom you have inherited hostile prejudices? How welcoming are you to exiles who seek refuge in this country? In your community? How would you respond to a relationship developing between a refugee and a member of your family?

3. The story of Ruth might perhaps be compared with the Gospel story of the Good Samaritan (Luke 10:29-37). The person who does the will of God is a foreigner, of a nation despised by many as ethnically impure and not true worshippers of God. How do we relate to foreigners, "others", in our society? Do we judge their moral character on the basis of racial and religious stereotypes? What is the source of the information on which our prejudices are based? Are there experiences we can identify in our own lives where we have

received God's blessings through the words and actions of people from whom we would least expect it?

4. The story of Ruth gleaning grain in Boaz's field illustrates both the vulnerability of women to molestation and exploitation, and indirectly the suspicion and blame that are often attached to women who are victims of sexual aggression. How do we recognize those who are vulnerable in our communities? Are we too inclined to blame them as "seductive" or "provocative", particularly if they are outsiders to our community, and the perpetrators are people like us?

5. As David's great-grandmother, Ruth is an ancestor of the royal line of Judah. Therefore, as the Gospel of Matthew points out, she is an ancestor of Jesus. So too is Rahab, the Canaanite prostitute of Jericho who sheltered the spies sent by Joshua (Joshua 2), and who became the mother of Boaz (Matthew 1:5). What does this tell us about the ways in which God's purposes are worked out in the world? Are we willing to accept people we might regard as outcasts, immoral or otherwise tainted, and to recognize that God may be using them in a quite distinct way?

Points for prayer

1. People driven by circumstance to leave their homes and livelihood behind them, and to find refuge in strange countries with very different cultures, especially where the host society is unwelcoming and hostile.
2. Women who are vulnerable, especially when alone in a strange place, and are liable to be blamed for crimes of which they are victims.
3. The people of Bethlehem, especially those who have been driven from their homes through encroachment by Israeli settlements and the Separation Wall, and refugees from elsewhere in Palestine who find shelter in Aida, D'heisheh, and Beit Jibrin camps.

Samuel anointing David. Samuel van Hoogstraten (1627–78), Städel Museum, Frankfurt am Main. Public domain.

3

David

David is one of the great heroes of the Old Testament, a warrior who reigned as king and conquered Jerusalem during the period *c*.1000–960 BC. Because of his military prowess, and his dynasty which ruled from Jerusalem for centuries, David has been a symbol of future hope in some strands of Judaism. Particularly in times of crisis and oppression, movements emerged of Jewish people who awaited a king like David, who would arise and deliver Israel from foreign tyranny, and re-establish its political and military power. Christians of course see these expectations transformed and fulfilled in Jesus, whose saving work and kingly rule embrace all humanity, far transcending nationalist chauvinism of any kind. For Muslims, David is a prophet, the supreme earthly ruler, *khalifa*:

> David, We have given you mastery over the land. Judge fairly between people. Do not follow your desires, lest they divert you from God's path:

those who wander from His path will have a
painful torment because they ignore the Day of
Reckoning (*Qur'an* 38, *Sad* 26).

He is also the recipient of *zabur*, divine revelations corresponding to the Psalms in Jewish and Christian Scripture. God addresses Muhammed thus:

> We have sent revelation to you [Prophet] as
> We did to Noah and the prophets after him, to
> Abraham, Ishmael, Isaac, Jacob, and the Tribes,
> to Jesus, Job, Jonah, Aaron, and Solomon—to
> David We gave the book [of Psalms] (*Qur'an* 4,
> *An-Nisa* 163).

> Your Lord knows best about everyone in the
> heavens and the earth. We gave some prophets
> more than others: We gave David a book [of
> Psalms] (*Qur'an* 17, *Al-Isra* 55).

For Christians, the Psalms are also associated with David, and some are explicitly attributed to him in the biblical text. But perhaps David is remembered more particularly as the boy who killed the Philistine warrior Goliath with a slingshot, before himself becoming a warrior and the founder of a royal dynasty; most importantly, David is remembered as an ancestor of Jesus—whose kingship is fundamentally different to the military power of David. The youngest son of Jesse, the grandson of Boaz and Ruth (Ruth 4:17), is tending sheep in the fields which then surrounded Bethlehem, when Samuel comes to the town to anoint a king to take the place of Saul (1 Samuel 16). David is not called to the feast until Samuel has discerned that the son of Jesse whom God has chosen is none of the seven who had hitherto been presented to him:

> The Lord said to Samuel, "How long will you grieve over Saul? I have rejected him from being king over Israel. Fill your horn with oil and set out; I will send you to Jesse the Bethlehemite, for I have provided for myself a king among his sons." Samuel said, "How can I go? If Saul hears of it, he will kill me." And the Lord said, "Take a heifer with you, and say, "I have come to sacrifice to the Lord." Invite Jesse to the sacrifice, and I will show you what you shall do; and you shall anoint for me the one whom I name to you." Samuel did what the Lord commanded, and came to Bethlehem. The elders of the city came to meet him trembling, and said, "Do you come peaceably?" He said, "Peaceably; I have come to sacrifice to the Lord; sanctify yourselves and come with me to the sacrifice." And he sanctified Jesse and his sons and invited them to the sacrifice. When they came, he looked on Eliab and thought, "Surely the Lord's anointed is now before the Lord." But the Lord said to Samuel,

"Do not look on his appearance or on the height of his stature, because I have rejected him; for the Lord does not see as mortals see; they look on the outward appearance, but the Lord looks on the heart." Then Jesse called Abinadab, and made him pass before Samuel. He said, "Neither has the Lord chosen this one." Then Jesse made Shammah pass by. And he said, "Neither has the Lord chosen this one." Jesse made seven of his sons pass before Samuel, and Samuel said to Jesse, "The Lord has not chosen any of these." Samuel said to Jesse, "Are all your sons here?" And he said, "There remains yet the youngest, but he is keeping the sheep." And Samuel said to Jesse, "Send and bring him; for we will not sit down until he comes here." He sent and brought him in. Now he was ruddy, and had beautiful eyes, and was handsome. The Lord said, "Rise and anoint him; for this is the one." Then Samuel took the horn of oil, and anointed him in the presence of his brothers; and the spirit of the Lord came mightily upon David from that day forward. Samuel then set out and went to Ramah (1 Samuel 16:1-13).

The olive oil with which kings, priests and others are ritually inaugurated in ancient Israel is a sign of God's Spirit, the power by which they will do the work for which they have been set apart. The Hebrew word for anoint is *moshaḥ*, from which the word messiah, anointed one, is derived. Similarly, the Greek word for oil, *chrisma*, is derived from *chrio*, the verb meaning to anoint, as is *christos*, the anointed one, from which we derive the word Christ. The oil used for anointing at Baptism, and at Ordination, and on other occasions in some churches, is called chrism, from the same word. The word Christ originated as a descriptive title of the one anointed by God, before becoming in effect a name of Jesus.

One site in Bethlehem traditionally associated with David is a series of ancient water cisterns, rediscovered in 1895 and still in use, known today as King David's Wells. The story is told of David and his troops, encamped in a cave or fortress at Adullam, to the west of Bethlehem, while the Philistines were occupying the town:

> Towards the beginning of harvest three of the thirty chiefs went down to join David at the cave of Adullam, while a band of Philistines was encamped in the valley of Rephaim. David was then in the stronghold; and the garrison of the Philistines was then at Bethlehem. David said longingly, "O that someone would give me water to drink from the well of Bethlehem that is by the gate!" Then the three warriors broke through the camp of the Philistines, drew water from the well of Bethlehem that was by the gate, and brought it to David. But he would not drink

of it; he poured it out to the Lord, for he said,
"The Lord forbid that I should do this. Can I
drink the blood of the men who went at the risk
of their lives?" Therefore he would not drink it.
The three warriors did these things (2 Samuel
23:13-17).

The Philistines were a regional superpower, living in and around cities of the Mediterranean coast. At times, they had dominated and oppressed the people of the interior, including the tribes of Israel and Judah, and there was longstanding enmity, as is reflected in the story of Samson (Judges 13-16) as well as of Saul and David (1-2 Samuel). In the hearing of his soldiers, David expresses a yearning to drink from the well at the town gate of Bethlehem. This was probably intended as a figurative statement of his desire to liberate the town from the Philistines. Three of his soldiers nonetheless took him literally, and demonstrated their courage and loyalty, either by stealing into the town surreptitiously or by engaging the garrison in combat, and drawing water from the well, which they brought to David. He refused to drink, equating the water with the blood of those who had risked their lives to obtain it. David accordingly offers the water as a sacrifice to God.

Water is a scarce resource in Bethlehem today, and more widely in Palestine. While the land is prone to droughts, normal rainfall is abundant, but seasonal. Subterranean aquifers supply wells, which used normally to provide sufficient water during the dry season. Modern technology has enabled water to be piped from the Sea of Galilee and the Jordan River, but this and water from the aquifers which feed wells, such as those in Bethlehem, are monopolized by Israeli settlements for agricultural and domestic use, as well as for gardens and swimming pools. Meanwhile, water supplies in Palestinian towns and cities are often limited to only a few hours a week or less, and wells run dry on account of over-exploitation of the aquifers. Tanks for rainwater capture and hydroponic systems[1] are frequently shot at or otherwise vandalized by Israeli forces in gratuitous acts of destruction, with the intention of causing thirst to humans and animals, and the hunger and other health problems it causes.

David is remembered as the boy who killed the Philistine soldier Goliath with a stone shot from his sling:

> The Philistine came on and drew near to David, with his shield-bearer in front of him. When the Philistine looked and saw David, he disdained him, for he was only a youth, ruddy and handsome in appearance. The Philistine said to David, "Am I a dog, that you come to me with sticks?" And the Philistine cursed David by

---

[1] Hydroponic technologies grow plants without soil, using minimal quantities of water, and providing nutrients by other means, enabling the production of food crops where land and water are scarce.

his gods. The Philistine said to David, "Come to me, and I will give your flesh to the birds of the air and to the wild animals of the field." But David said to the Philistine, "You come to me with sword and spear and javelin; but I come to you in the name of the Lord of hosts, the God of the armies of Israel, whom you have defied. This very day the Lord will deliver you into my hand, and I will strike you down and cut off your head; and I will give the dead bodies of the Philistine army this very day to the birds of the air and to the wild animals of the earth, so that all the earth may know that there is a God in Israel, and that all this assembly may know that the Lord does not save by sword and spear; for the battle is the Lord's and he will give you into our hand." When the Philistine drew nearer to meet David, David ran quickly towards the battle line to meet the Philistine. David put his hand in his bag, took out a stone, slung it, and struck the Philistine on his forehead; the stone sank into his forehead, and he fell face down on the ground (1 Samuel 17:41-49).

This story is related also in the Qur'an:

> When Talut[2] set out with his forces, he said to them, "God will test you with a river. Anyone

---
[2] Saul.

who drinks from it will not belong with me, but anyone who refrains from tasting it will belong with me; if he scoops up just one handful [he will be excused]." But they all drank [deep] from it, except for a few. When he crossed it with those who had kept faith, they said, "We have no strength today against Goliath and his warriors." But those who knew that they were going to meet their Lord said, "How often a small force has defeated a large army with God's permission! God is with those who are steadfast." And when they met Goliath and his warriors, they said, "Our Lord, pour patience on us, make us stand firm, and help us against the disbelievers," and so with God's permission they defeated them. David killed Goliath, and God gave him sovereignty and wisdom and taught him what He pleased. If God did not drive some back by means of others the earth would be completely corrupt, but God is bountiful to all (*Qur'an* 2, *Al-Baqarah* 249-51).

David went on to become a successful soldier, who led his army to victory against the oppressors and enemies of his people. In due course, following the death of Saul, he became king (2 Samuel 2:4), expanded the national borders, and subjected neighbouring people to his rule. The ascription of David as *khalifa* in the *Qur'an* (Surah 38, *Sad* 26) derives from this tradition. The Arabic word *khalifa* means vicegerent and denotes the supreme earthly ruler in Islam.

David is remembered also as a musician, who played the harp or lyre:

> Now the spirit of the Lord departed from Saul, and an evil spirit from the Lord tormented him. And Saul's servants said to him, "See now, an evil spirit from God is tormenting you. Let our lord now command the servants who attend you to look for someone who is skilful in playing the lyre; and when the evil spirit from God is upon you, he will play it, and you will feel better." So Saul said to his servants, "Provide for me someone who can play well, and bring him to me." One of the young men answered, "I have seen a son of Jesse the Bethlehemite who is skilful in playing, a man of valour, a warrior, prudent in speech, and a man of good presence; and the Lord is with him." So Saul sent messengers to Jesse, and said, "Send me your son David who is with the sheep." Jesse took a donkey loaded with bread, a skin of wine, and a kid, and sent them by his son David to Saul. And David came to Saul, and entered his service. Saul loved him greatly, and he became his armour-bearer. Saul sent to Jesse, saying, "Let David remain in my service, for he has found favour in my sight." And whenever the evil spirit from God came

upon Saul, David took the lyre and played it with his hand, and Saul would be relieved and feel better, and the evil spirit would depart from him (1 Samuel 16:14-23).

Many of the psalms still sung in Christian as well as Jewish worship are attributed to David; this is understood not merely as reflecting natural aptitude, but inspiration from God, so that David's words may have the status of prophecy. In Islam, David is the recipient of God's revelation in the *Zabur* (*Qur'an* 4, *An-Nisa* 163; 17, *Al-Isra* 55). While no Islamic text of the *Zabur* survives, the Psalms preserved in Jewish and Christian Bibles are understood to be derived from the *Zabur*, rather than as preserving intact God's revelation to David. Jews and Christians cannot accept this reconstruction, for which there is no historical or textual evidence. It is nevertheless important that we recognize that, for nearly 1,400 years, Muslims have held these convictions about David.

Despite the difficulties which afflicted him, and his own shortcomings, David is remembered in the biblical tradition as having remained faithful to God. God in return promised that David's descendants would rule over Israel for ever:

> Your house and your kingdom shall be made sure for ever before me; your throne shall be established for ever (2 Samuel 7:16).

The subsequent history is very different. The tenuous unity which David maintained at great cost became strained as the rule of his son Solomon became increasingly despotic and oppressive (1 Kings 3-11). Solomon's son Rehoboam alienated the northern tribes entirely (1 Kings 12), and a rival kingdom of Israel emerged, separated from and often at enmity with David's descendants, the kings of Judah:

> When all Israel saw that the king would not listen to them, the people answered the king,
> 'What share do we have in David?
> We have no inheritance in the son of Jesse.
> To your tents, O Israel!
> Look now to your own house, O David.'
> So Israel went away to their tents. But Rehoboam reigned over the Israelites who were living in the towns of Judah. When King Rehoboam sent Adoram, who was taskmaster over the forced labour, all Israel stoned him to death. King Rehoboam then hurriedly mounted his chariot to flee to Jerusalem. So Israel has been in rebellion against the house of David to this day (1 Kings 12:16-19).

The kingdom of Israel was ruled by a succession of dynasties from Shechem and then from Samaria for 200 years before being overthrown by the Assyrians:

> In the fourth year of King Hezekiah, which was the seventh year of King Hoshea son of Elah of Israel, King Shalmaneser of Assyria came up against Samaria, besieged it, and at the end of three years took it. In the sixth year of Hezekiah, which was the ninth year of King Hoshea of Israel, Samaria was taken (2 Kings 18:9-10).

Assyria was one of the superpowers of the ancient world, ruling from Nineveh in Mesopotamia. Following the division of the kingdom, David's descendants ruled a very much smaller and weaker kingdom from Jerusalem for 400 years, before they were overthrown by the Babylonians, another Mesopotamian superpower which overthrew the Assyrians and established an empire which extended to the frontiers of Egypt:

> In his days King Nebuchadnezzar of Babylon came up; Jehoiakim became his servant for three years; then he turned and rebelled against him. The Lord sent against him bands of the Chaldeans, bands of the Arameans, bands of the Moabites, and bands of the Ammonites; he sent them against Judah to destroy it, according to the word of the Lord that he spoke by his servants the prophets. Surely this came upon Judah at the command of the Lord, to remove them out of his sight, for the sins of Manasseh, for all that he had committed, and also for the

innocent blood that he had shed; for he filled Jerusalem with innocent blood, and the Lord was not willing to pardon (2 Kings 24:1-4).

At that time the servants of King Nebuchadnezzar of Babylon came up to Jerusalem, and the city was besieged. King Nebuchadnezzar of Babylon came to the city, while his servants were besieging it; King Jehoiachin of Judah gave himself up to the king of Babylon, himself, his mother, his servants, his officers, and his palace officials. The king of Babylon took him prisoner in the eighth year of his reign. He carried off all the treasures of the house of the Lord, and the treasures of the king's house; he cut in pieces all the vessels of gold in the temple of the Lord, which King Solomon of Israel had made, all this as the Lord had foretold. He carried away all Jerusalem, all the officials, all the warriors, ten thousand captives, all the artisans and the smiths; no one remained, except the poorest people of the land. He carried away Jehoiachin to Babylon; the king's mother, the king's wives, his officials, and the elite of the land, he took into captivity from Jerusalem to Babylon. The king of Babylon brought captive to Babylon all the men of valour, seven thousand, the artisans and the smiths, one thousand, all of them strong and fit for war (2 Kings 24:10-16).

And in the ninth year of his reign, in the tenth month, on the tenth day of the month, King Nebuchadnezzar of Babylon came with all his army against Jerusalem, and laid siege to it; they built siege-works against it all round. So the city was besieged until the eleventh year of King Zedekiah. On the ninth day of the fourth month the famine became so severe in the city that there was no food for the people of the land. Then a breach was made in the city wall; the king with all the soldiers fled by night by the way of the gate between the two walls, by the king's garden, though the Chaldeans were all round the city. They went in the direction of the Arabah. But the army of the Chaldeans pursued the king, and overtook him in the plains of Jericho; all his army was scattered, deserting him. Then they captured the king and brought him up to the king of Babylon at Riblah, who passed sentence on him. They slaughtered the sons of Zedekiah before his eyes, then put out the eyes of Zedekiah; they bound him in fetters and took him to Babylon (2 Kings 25:1-7).

In the fifth month, on the seventh day of the month—which was the nineteenth year of King Nebuchadnezzar, king of Babylon—Nebuzaradan, the captain of the bodyguard, a servant of the king of Babylon, came to Jerusalem.

> He burned the house of the Lord, the king's house, and all the houses of Jerusalem; every great house he burned down. All the army of the Chaldeans who were with the captain of the guard broke down the walls around Jerusalem. Nebuzaradan the captain of the guard carried into exile the rest of the people who were left in the city and the deserters who had defected to the king of Babylon—all the rest of the population. But the captain of the guard left some of the poorest people of the land to be vine-dressers and tillers of the soil (2 Kings 25:8-12).

After the Babylonian empire was conquered by the Medo-Persians, Jerusalem and the temple were rebuilt, as we read in the books of Ezra and Nehemiah and see reflected in the prophets Haggai and Zechariah. While Sheshbazzar and Zerubbabel, the first two rulers of the province *Yehud Medinata*, were descended from the house of David, the royal vassals were soon replaced by a succession of governors who were imperial officials. Hopes were nonetheless sustained that God would in due time restore the dynasty of David, to rise against foreign oppressors and re-establish the kingdom, not merely to its former territories, but as a superpower dominating the Middle East:

> He will raise a signal for the nations, and will assemble the outcasts of Israel, and gather the

> dispersed of Judah from the four corners of the earth (Isaiah 11:12).
>
> My servant David shall be king over them; and they shall all have one shepherd. They shall follow my ordinances and be careful to observe my statutes (Ezekiel 37:24).
>
> Now you are walled around with a wall; siege is laid against us; with a rod they strike the ruler of Israel upon the cheek. But you, O Bethlehem of Ephrathah, who are one of the little clans of Judah, from you shall come forth for me one who is to rule in Israel, whose origin is from of old, from ancient days (Micah 5:1-2).
>
> And I will pour out a spirit of compassion and supplication on the house of David and the inhabitants of Jerusalem, so that, when they look on the one whom they have pierced, they shall mourn for him, as one mourns for an only child, and weep bitterly over him, as one weeps over a firstborn (Zechariah 12:10).

The hopes reflected in the Prophets developed during the centuries when Judaea was under Persian, Greek, Hasmonaean and Roman rule. The Persian empire was conquered by the Macedonian Alexander "the Great" in a series of campaigns 334-324 BC. After Alexander's death, his empire was divided and Judaea formed part of the Ptolemaic empire (based in Egypt) until 200 BC, when it passed to the Seleucid empire (based in Syria). Through the Maccabean Revolt (165–145 BC), Judaea progressively gained autonomy and ultimately independence under a priestly dynasty, the Hasmonaeans, who conquered the surrounding areas of Samaria, Galilee, Idumaea and Peraea. Dynastic disputes and the expansion of the Roman empire ended this independence by 67 BC, and an Idumaean family, the Herods, emerged as powerful agents of Roman rule in the Levant for over a century. The Herod who appears in Matthew 2, and is mentioned in Luke 1–2, ruled as king of the Jews from 37–4 BC. He was a loyal and effective vassal of Rome, and a notorious tyrant whose brutality is told not only in Matthew's nativity narrative but, more extensively, by the Jewish historian Josephus.

During this entire period, neither Jewish nor foreign rulers established justice or brought the peace and prosperity which would satisfy the people's hopes. Many accordingly hoped and prayed that God would intervene to restore the royal line of David, and establish a king who would rule in accordance with God's law, a messiah. This was the world into which Jesus was born, nearly a thousand years after David.

While Jesus was born into a society in which at least some hoped for the restoration of David's family to reign as kings over an independent and powerful nation, if we are to understand how Jesus fulfilled these hopes in quite unexpected ways, we need also to understand why the figure of David is more problematic than we may be tempted to assume.

When the elders of Israel came to Samuel, and asked him to appoint a king to replace the patterns of leadership which had prevailed under the Judges, Samuel's response was:

> These will be the ways of the king who will reign over you: he will take your sons and appoint them to his chariots and to be his horsemen, and to run before his chariots; and he will appoint for himself commanders of thousands and commanders of fifties, and some to plough his ground and to reap his harvest, and to make his implements of war and the equipment of his chariots. He will take your daughters to be perfumers and cooks and bakers. He will take the best of your fields and vineyards and olive orchards and give them to his courtiers. He will take one-tenth of your grain and of your vineyards and give it to his officers and his courtiers. He will take your male and female slaves, and the best of your cattle and donkeys, and put them to his work. He will take one-tenth of your flocks, and you shall be his slaves. And in that day you will cry out because of your king, whom you have chosen for yourselves; but the Lord will not answer you in that day (1 Samuel 8:11-18).

The subsequent history of Israel was very much as Samuel described. Far from being an agency for liberty and justice, the monarchy became an instrument of oppression and exploitation that consumed the resources of the land which God had given for the enjoyment of all. Taxation, land confiscation, conscription, and forced labour reduced many people to poverty or slavery, and incurred God's wrath—as articulated by the Prophets.

The first king, Saul, started well, but failed to keep to the law of God as Samuel had directed. David's successors were, with few exceptions, noted for turning away from God, depending on diplomatic, economic and military treaties with more powerful neighbours, and leading Israel into idolatry, the worship of the gods of the nations around them. David himself is far from consistently righteous. He is shown to be ruthless and vindictive in his dealings with real or perceived rivals, while indulgent towards his family in ways which bring enormous suffering on the people: the rebellion of his son Absalom, which led to destructive civil war, would not have taken place had David acted more responsibly, and sooner, in dealing with sexual abuse within his family (2 Samuel 13; 16-19). David abuses his power to take advantage of a woman married to one of his soldiers, and to arrange her husband's death in battle when he learns that she is pregnant (2 Samuel 11-12). The one area in which David is consistent and careful is in establishing the prerogatives of the monarchy, and the inviolability of the person of "the Lord's anointed".

Much of the narrative of David's reign in 2 Samuel 9–20, in fact, recounts his failures in judgement and in moral rectitude, and the sometimes terrible consequences for the nation he had been anointed to rule.

David's achievements were essentially military. From the killing of Goliath, through his career as a soldier in King Saul's army, his life as a bandit, mercenary and warlord, to his campaigns as king, he was "a man of war who has shed blood"—for which reason he was forbidden to build a temple in Jerusalem (1 Chronicles 28:3). The security against external enemies was attained not only at an immediate cost in human lives, but also at the long-term cost of maintaining an army and building and maintaining fortifications. Buildings were constructed with forced labour, and the armies and their horses sustained through heavy taxation. The social ethos of ancient Israel, as envisaged in God's revelation of the Law to Moses and implemented under the Judges, was eroded. The political dispensation David established did not last, but led to social and economic deterioration in the circumstances of nearly all the people he ruled. Israel and Judah ceased to be just societies, and for centuries the Prophets railed against evil and oppression, until Samaria and Jerusalem were both destroyed.

Questions for discussion

1. David is a heroic figure in Jewish, Christian and Muslim traditions. Yet he emerges from the pages of the Old Testament as a deeply flawed character. How do David's faults and failings affect your understanding of his place in God's saving work in the history of Israel? How does it affect your understanding of Jesus as David's heir? Can you draw comfort from God's choosing such a person, and others like David—perhaps people like us—to do God's work in the world?
2. David's reign saw military victories, attained at considerable social and economic cost, as well, no doubt, at the cost of the lives of his and his enemies' soldiers. Conscription, forced labour, and the accumulation of land, wealth and power by the king, his family and his retainers brought about corrosion of the core values of ancient Israelite society. What does this say about recourse to force and violence to achieve what may seem just and reasonable objectives?
3. David is remembered as a military figure, a successful soldier who became a mighty king. For some Jews of later centuries, the messiah would be another king, like David, and perhaps his descendant, who would bring liberty through military power. For others, the messiah would be a prophet, one like Moses who would create a

new society, a faithful servant of God who would suffer greatly on account of human sinfulness. The Christian understanding of Jesus has drawn from all these traditions. While Jesus firmly rejected military power and violence as a means of creating his kingdom, Christians have not always been unwilling to use force to attain their objectives. What does the example of David teach us about the perils of relying on human power to achieve even the most worthy and righteous of goals?

4. The fields around Bethlehem in which David tended his father's sheep are now covered in Israeli settlements and the homes of Palestinian refugees expelled from their lands over the last century. Some fields are cut off from Bethlehem by the Separation Wall. Those fields are no longer available for the people of Bethlehem to graze their animals or to grow olive and fruit trees. Can you identify with the frustration and anger felt by people who have been forcibly deprived of their land, homes and livelihood? Can you understand the urge to meet violence with violence, especially when nurtured by the story of David's overcoming seemingly greater power by the use of force and guile? Can you appreciate the despair of those who feel they have no other option?

5. Given what you have learned about Bethlehem, and about Palestine, how would you hope that

God will act to bring justice and peace? What messiah would you seek?

Points for prayer

1. The people of Bethlehem, and elsewhere in Palestine and around the world, who have lost homes and livelihood through violent expulsion, especially those who bear the additional emotional cost of having lost land tended by their families for generations, and whose loved ones were killed or maimed when they were driven from their homes and land.
2. All who thirst on account of the shortage of water, and who watch their crops and animals die for lack of water; those who go hungry on account of the shortage of food which results.
3. All who are tempted to resort to violence to defend themselves, their families and their homes, or to reclaim that which they have lost through violence.
4. People in positions of leadership and authority, especially in Palestine, who face the daily temptations of corruption and abuse of power, and those who are exploited and abused by their leaders and others with power over them.
5. All who await this Advent the fulfilment of God's promises, that hope may be kept alive in times of trouble and uncertainty.

Elijah fed by ravens. Mural in Mar Elias Monastery, Bethlehem. Photograph: Bukvoed via Wikimedia Commons (CC BY 4.0).

4

Elijah

Alongside the road northwards from Bethlehem towards Jerusalem, on the "green line" which marks the internationally recognized border between Israel and Palestine, lies the Greek Orthodox Monastery of Mar Elias. Now cut off from Bethlehem, and from the people whose forebears, Christian and Muslim alike, have worshipped there for centuries, by the Separation Wall, the monastery is surrounded no longer by orchards and olive groves but by the Jewish settlements of Gilo and Har Homa.

Mar Elias is an Aramaic or Syriac rendering of the Greek 'Agios Elias; *mar* or *'agios* meaning holy or, as we would say in that context, Saint. Elias is the Greek rendering of the Hebrew Eliyahu, from which derives the English Elijah. In Eastern Orthodoxy, the patriarchs and prophets of the Old Testament are revered as saints, alongside the apostles and other "saints" of the New Testament and early Church. While Elijah is not alone among figures of ancient Israel who are revered as saints and commemorated in the calendar and in the dedication of churches, he does have a very particular significance in both the Old and New Testaments. Elijah is one of three figures in the Old Testament whose death is somewhat mysterious.

The first is Enoch, one of the forebears of Noah about whom only a few verses are written in Scripture, the most significant being:

> Enoch walked with God; then he was no more, because God took him (Genesis 5:24).

The significance of this enigmatic statement was to become the subject of a great deal of reflection and speculation during the centuries surrounding the birth of Jesus. Enoch is mentioned in the letter to the Hebrews:

> By faith Enoch was taken so that he did not experience death; and "he was not found, because God had taken him." For it was attested before he was taken away that "he had pleased God". And without faith it is impossible to please God, for whoever would approach him must believe that he exists and that he rewards those who seek him (Hebrews 11:5-6).

These brief allusions to a much larger tradition can easily be overlooked by modern Christians, for whom the traditions surrounding Enoch are largely forgotten.

The book known in western Christian Pseudepigrapha[1] as 1 Enoch continues to be revered as Scripture in the Ethiopian and Eritrean Orthodox Churches, and was clearly widely read in Judaism of the time of Jesus. Copies of this book were found among the Dead Sea Scrolls at Qumran,[2] and the book is cited in the New Testament letter of Jude:

> It was also about these that Enoch, in the seventh generation from Adam, prophesied, saying, "See, the Lord is coming with tens of thousands of his holy ones, to execute judgement on all, and to convict everyone of all the deeds of ungodliness that they have committed in such an ungodly way, and of all the harsh things that ungodly sinners have spoken against him" (Jude 14-15, citing 1 Enoch 60:8).

1 Enoch was revered as Scripture by several early Christian writers and is still read as Scripture in the Ethiopian Orthodox Tewahedo Church—and by

---

[1] Pseudepigrapha are collections of texts which do not form part of the Canon of Scripture in the western Christian Churches but have been read and revered as Scripture by some Jewish or Christian groups in antiquity, and in some cases to the present day.

[2] Qumran, on the western shore of the Dead Sea, is the location of a series of caves in which deposits of ancient manuscripts, commonly known as the Dead Sea Scrolls, were discovered in 1947. These are generally associated with the ruins of a nearby settlement, commonly identified as that of a Jewish sect known as the Essenes.

Ethiopian Beta[3] Jews. The figure of Enoch was deemed significant by the first Christians, and continues to be so regarded among their descendants, precisely because of his not having died a natural death. The visions attributed to him in the book that bears his name were understood in some way to point to Jesus.

Secondly, Moses, the mediator of the Law and antecedent of the Prophets, whose death and burial are reported at the conclusion of the narrative of Israel's desert wanderings, prior to the invasion and conquest of Canaan under Joshua's leadership:

> Then Moses, the servant of the Lord, died there in the land of Moab, at the Lord's command. He was buried in a valley in the land of Moab, opposite Beth-peor, but no one knows his burial place to this day (Deuteronomy 34:5-6).

While the text does not actually say so, it came to be understood to mean that God had buried Moses out of human sight. Burial needs to be understood not simply as the act of digging a grave and depositing the body before filling the hole again, but rather the whole process of transition from the end of earthly life to existence which follows death. As the ideas of resurrection and

---

[3] Israeli agents have orchestrated a wave of migrations of Ethiopian Jews to Israel, where they have become an underclass, whose dark skins are cause for discrimination in a society dominated by Jews of European extraction, and whose status as Jews is disputed by some rabbinic authorities.

afterlife crystallized in Jewish tradition many centuries later, this text was to become the subject of speculation, as was the expectation that God would in the future raise up another prophet like Moses:

> The Lord your God will raise up for you a prophet like me from among your own people; you shall heed such a prophet. This is what you requested of the Lord your God at Horeb on the day of the assembly when you said: "If I hear the voice of the Lord my God any more, or ever again see this great fire, I will die." Then the Lord replied to me: 'They are right in what they have said. I will raise up for them a prophet like you from among their own people; I will put my words in the mouth of the prophet, who shall speak to them everything that I command. Anyone who does not heed the words that the prophet shall speak in my name, I myself will hold accountable (Deuteronomy 18:15-19).

Like Enoch, Moses is the subject of pseudepigraphical books, which were read as Scripture by some Jewish and Christian groups in antiquity.

Elijah is traditionally identified as the first of the great prophets of Israel, the predecessor of those who were later to leave oracles and narrative accounts of events in their ministries, which were to be compiled into the books which bear their names. Elijah and his immediate successor, Elisha, left no such literary legacy, but he is nonetheless remembered as the archetypal prophet, and was to be the subject of later pseudepigrapha. Elijah's ministry concludes with the dramatic account of his being taken up into heaven in a fiery chariot, one of the most extraordinary events recorded in the Hebrew Scriptures:

> Now when the Lord was about to take Elijah up to heaven by a whirlwind, Elijah and Elisha were on their way from Gilgal. Elijah said to Elisha, "Stay here; for the Lord has sent me as far as Bethel." But Elisha said, "As the Lord lives, and as you yourself live, I will not leave you." So they went down to Bethel. The company of prophets who were in Bethel came out to Elisha, and said to him, "Do you know that today the Lord will take your master away from you?" And he said, "Yes, I know; keep silent."
>
> Elijah said to him, "Elisha, stay here; for the Lord has sent me to Jericho." But he said, "As the Lord lives, and as you yourself live, I will not leave you." So they came to Jericho. The company of prophets who were at Jericho drew near to Elisha, and said to him, "Do you know that today the Lord will take your master away from you?" And he answered, "Yes, I know; be silent."

Then Elijah said to him, "Stay here; for the Lord has sent me to the Jordan." But he said, "As the Lord lives, and as you yourself live, I will not leave you." So the two of them went on. Fifty men of the company of prophets also went, and stood at some distance from them, as they both were standing by the Jordan. Then Elijah took his mantle and rolled it up, and struck the water; the water was parted to the one side and to the other, until the two of them crossed on dry ground.

When they had crossed, Elijah said to Elisha, "Tell me what I may do for you, before I am taken from you." Elisha said, "Please let me inherit a double share of your spirit." He responded, "You have asked a hard thing; yet, if you see me as I am being taken from you, it will be granted you; if not, it will not." As they continued walking and talking, a chariot of fire and horses of fire separated the two of them, and Elijah ascended in a whirlwind into heaven. Elisha kept watching and crying out, "Father, father! The chariots of Israel and its horsemen!" But when he could no longer see him, he grasped his own clothes and tore them in two pieces.

He picked up the mantle of Elijah that had fallen from him, and went back and stood on the bank of the Jordan. He took the mantle of Elijah that had fallen from him, and struck the water, saying, "Where is the Lord, the God of Elijah?" When he had struck the water, the water was parted to the one side and to the other, and Elisha went over.

When the company of prophets who were at Jericho saw him at a distance, they declared, "The spirit of Elijah rests on Elisha." They came to meet him and bowed to the ground before him. They said to him, "See now, we have fifty strong men among your servants; please let them go and seek your master; it may be that the spirit of the Lord has caught him up and thrown him down on some mountain or into some valley." He responded, "No, do not send them." But when they urged him until he was ashamed, he said, "Send them." So they sent fifty men who searched for three days but did not find him. When they came back to him (he had remained at Jericho), he said to them, "Did I not say to you, Do not go?" (2 Kings 2:1-18).

This extraordinary phenomenon imbues Elijah with a particular significance and holiness, and in subsequent tradition developed into the expectation that, not having died, he would return to prepare Israel for the coming of God's judgement and deliverance:

> Remember the teaching of my servant Moses, the statutes and ordinances that I commanded him at Horeb for all Israel. Lo, I will send you the prophet Elijah before the great and terrible day of the Lord comes. He will turn the hearts of parents to their children and the hearts of children to their parents, so that I will not come and strike the land with a curse (Malachi 4:4-6).

These are, significantly for Christians, the closing words of the Old Testament, but we need to be aware that, in the Canon of Jewish Scripture, the books are arranged in a different order, so these words do not represent a transition from one epoch to another, and certainly not to the Christian New Testament. Nevertheless, it is significant that Moses and Elijah are here closely associated, but it is Elijah whose return is anticipated, preceding God's eschatological judgement.

In rabbinic tradition, Elijah's presence as a witness is anticipated at circumcisions, and a chair is accordingly provided for him. This relates to his role in upholding the Covenant of which circumcision is a sign. Some ancient rabbis maintained that Elijah's role in watching over the ritual is a penalty for his having overstated the degree to which the people of Israel had turned from God to idolatry, in a passage we will consider shortly (1 Kings 19:10,14). Similarly, a place, and a cup of wine, are set for Elijah at every Passover meal, during the course of which the door is opened, and he is invited to enter. The roots of this tradition lie in the interpretation of Malachi (quoted above), and the expectation that deliverance would come at Passover, the commemoration of Israel's deliverance from slavery in Egypt. Elijah was also looked upon as the eschatological arbiter of difficult questions on which the rabbis could not agree, and a decision would wait "until Elijah comes". The concluding prayer each sabbath, known as *Havdalah*, prays for the swift return of Elijah. This too derives from the expectation, first attested in Malachi, that Elijah would return to earth and play a distinctive role in God's eschatological restoration of Israel.

In the New Testament, Elijah appears alongside Moses, the mediator of the Law and the other principal figure from the Old Testament whose death is extraordinary, at the Transfiguration of Jesus:

> Six days later, Jesus took with him Peter and James and John, and led them up a high mountain apart, by themselves. And he was transfigured before them, and his clothes became dazzling white, such as no one on earth could bleach them. And there appeared to them Elijah with Moses, who were talking with Jesus. Then Peter said to Jesus, "Rabbi, it is good for us to be here; let us make three dwellings, one for you, one for Moses, and one for Elijah." He did not know what to say, for they were terrified. Then a cloud overshadowed them, and from the

cloud there came a voice, "This is my Son, the Beloved; listen to him!" Suddenly when they looked around, they saw no one with them any more, but only Jesus (Mark 9:2-8; see also Matthew 17:1-8; Luke 9:28-36).

The Law and the Prophets are shown to be fulfilled in Jesus, and in the saving work he was to accomplish through his death and resurrection. In the Gospels and later Christian tradition, it is understood that John the Baptist fulfils the eschatological role of Elijah, preparing for the coming of God's reign in and through Jesus. This is made clear in the appearance of the angel Gabriel to his father, Zechariah, in the temple:

> [Your child] will turn many of the people of Israel to the Lord their God. With the spirit and power of Elijah he will go before him, to turn the hearts of parents to their children, and the disobedient to the wisdom of the righteous, to make ready a people prepared for the Lord (Luke 1:16-17).

This identification is explicitly affirmed by Jesus:

> Truly I tell you, among those born of women no one has arisen greater than John the Baptist; yet the least in the kingdom of heaven is greater than he. From the days of John the Baptist

until now the kingdom of heaven has suffered violence, and the violent take it by force. For all the prophets and the law prophesied until John came; and if you are willing to accept it, he is Elijah who is to come (Matthew 11:11-14).

And the disciples asked [Jesus], "Why, then, do the scribes say that Elijah must come first?" He replied, "Elijah is indeed coming and will restore all things; but I tell you that Elijah has already come, and they did not recognize him, but they did to him whatever they pleased. So also the Son of Man is about to suffer at their hands." Then the disciples understood that he was speaking to them about John the Baptist (Matthew 17:10-13).

When John's messengers had gone, Jesus began to speak to the crowds about John: "What did you go out into the wilderness to look at? A reed shaken by the wind? What then did you go out to see? Someone dressed in soft robes? Look, those who put on fine clothing and live in luxury are in royal palaces. What then did you go out to see? A prophet? Yes, I tell you, and more than a prophet. This is the one about whom it is written, 'See, I am sending my messenger ahead of you, who will prepare your way before you'" (Luke 7:24-7).

This does not mean that the relationship between John and Jesus is uncomplicated, as is clear from the somewhat enigmatic opening statement in the first of the above quotations. According to Luke, Jesus and John are blood relations through their mothers, Mary and Elizabeth (Luke 1:36). It is also in Luke that we are told that John is, by implication, a priest (Luke 1).[4] The complexity of their relationship is evident in Gospel accounts of Jesus' seeking John's baptism:

> Then Jesus came from Galilee to John at the Jordan, to be baptized by him. John would have prevented him, saying, "I need to be baptized by you, and do you come to me?" But Jesus answered him, "Let it be so now; for it is proper for us in this way to fulfil all righteousness." Then he consented. And when Jesus had been baptized, just as he came up from the water, suddenly the heavens were opened to him and he saw the Spirit of God descending like a dove and alighting on him. And a voice from heaven said, "This is my Son, the Beloved, with whom I am well pleased" (Matthew 3:13-17; cf. Mark 1:9-11; Luke 3:21-2).

---

[4] Priesthood in Israel is hereditary and limited to those identified as male descendants of Aaron, Moses' brother. As Zechariah was a priest, his son John is born to that status and role in the temple. John is nowhere depicted officiating as a priest in the temple, but this status might nonetheless add significance to the baptism ritual he offered outside the temple.

It is apparent also in John's doubts about Jesus:

> When John heard in prison what the Messiah was doing, he sent word by his disciples and said to him, "Are you the one who is to come, or are we to wait for another?" Jesus answered them, "Go and tell John what you hear and see: the blind receive their sight, the lame walk, the lepers are cleansed, the deaf hear, the dead are raised, and the poor have good news brought to them. And blessed is anyone who takes no offence at me" (Matthew 11:2-6; cf. Luke 7:19-23).

While there is this ambivalence in the relationship between John and Jesus reflected in the Gospels, it remains clear that John is immensely significant, and his role is interpreted in terms of the expected return of Elijah to prepare for the coming of God's judgement.

In the Qur'an, Elijah (Ilyas) is identified as a prophet:

> "It is those who have faith, and do not mix their faith with idolatry, who will be secure, and it is they who are rightly guided." Such was the argument We gave to Abraham against his people—We raise in rank whoever We will—your Lord is all wise, all knowing. We gave him Isaac and Jacob, each of whom We guided, as We had guided Noah before, and among his

descendants were David, Solomon, Job, Joseph, Moses, and Aaron—in this way We reward those who do good—Zachariah, John, Jesus, and Elijah—every one of them was righteous—Ishmael, Elisha, Jonah, and Lot. We favoured each one of them over other people, and also some of their forefathers, their offspring, and their brothers: We chose them and guided them on a straight path. Such is God's guidance, with which He guides whichever of His servants He will. If they had associated other gods with Him, all their deeds would have come to nothing. Those are the ones to whom We gave the Scripture, wisdom, and prophethood. Even if these people now disbelieve in them, we have entrusted them to others who do not disbelieve. Those were the people God guided, "[Prophet], follow the guidance they received." Say, "I ask no reward for it from you: it is a lesson for all people" (Sura 6, *Al An'am* 82-90).

John and his father Zechariah, as well as Jesus and Elijah, are listed among figures of Hebrew Scripture and the Christian New Testament who have been guided by God. As in 1 Kings, Elijah is portrayed as a vigorous preacher against idolatry. While his message is rejected by the majority of his hearers, he is nonetheless identified as one of Allah's righteous and faithful servants:

> Elijah too was one of the messengers. He said to his people, "Have you no fear of God? How can you invoke Baal and forsake the Most Gracious Creator, God, your Lord and the Lord of your forefathers?" but they rejected him. They will be brought to punishment as a consequence; not so the true servants of God. We let him be praised by succeeding generations: "Peace be to Elijah!" This is how We reward those who do good: truly he was one of Our faithful servants (Sura 37, *Al-Saffat* 123-32).

Subsequent Muslim tradition links Elijah with John and Jesus, as do the Druze, an Arab people of the Levant whose distinct identity and belief system share many traditions common to Christianity and Islam. The expected eschatological return of Elijah, in the company of a figure known as *Khidr*, sometimes identified with the angelic figure who explains mysteries to Moses/Musa (Sura 18, *Al-Kahf* 65-82), to play a role in God's judgement is also attested in some strands of Islamic thought.

Nowhere in the Elijah narrative in 1 Kings is Bethlehem named. Elijah's prophetic ministry was located in the northern kingdom of Israel, and he is associated primarily with Mount Carmel and the royal city of Samaria. Like John the Baptist, Elijah also has associations with the desert, but as a place of refuge rather than the location of his prophetic ministry. It was while fleeing the wrath and vengeance of Jezebel, queen of Israel, after his contest with the prophets of Ba'al on Mount Carmel, ending in their slaughter (1 Kings 18), that, according to tradition, Elijah rested at Bethlehem. Mar Elias Monastery, according to this tradition, marks the place of Elijah's temporary refuge on his way, via Beer-Sheba, to Horeb (Sinai), where he was to meet God. According to the narrative in 1 Kings 19, an angel appears to Elijah as he rests and provides him with food and drink for the journey, and God's word guides him to the summit of the mountain. There Elijah meets God in quite dramatic ways, evocative of the accounts of Moses' meeting with God at the summit of Mount Sinai in Exodus, but also quite different: God is encountered, not in the storm, the earthquake or the fire, but in what is frequently rendered "a still small voice" or a "gentle whisper", but would more accurately be translated, somewhat paradoxically, "a sound of sheer silence". It is not that the sound is weak or still, but rather that the silence itself is palpable and powerful: the violent noise and destructive force of the wind, earthquake and fire give way to the silence and stillness in which God's presence may be perceived—just as in the first creation narrative in Genesis God brings order out of chaos.

Elijah is not to enjoy the peace of God's presence for longer than it requires to receive his instructions: he is to return to the turbulence of human society, and to generate further turbulence. He is commissioned to anoint in God's name—the word *mishakh*, from which messiah derives, is used three times—Ben-Hadad as king of Aram (Syria), Jehu as king of Israel, and Elisha as the prophet to succeed him. In other words, Elijah is to instigate in God's name military coups to overthrow the reigning monarchs of two kingdoms, as well as to prepare the way for his prophetic ministry to be continued.

Prophecy, as epitomized by Elijah, is not simply foretelling the future from a position of comfort. It is speaking and acting in God's name and playing a part in the fulfilment of God's purposes. Speaking in God's name always means pronouncing God's judgement—if all is well in human society there is no occasion for God's intervention or for the work of prophecy. Those in power are condemned for their abuse of the privileged positions they occupy, and those afflicted hear words of comfort, not necessarily of immediate relief of their suffering, but of assurance that God's purposes would be brought to completion, in God's time, and in God's way. This does not mean that human beings have no part to play; indeed, Elijah is called not merely to speak, but to act, instigating revolution in two powerful kingdoms, in order that God's justice may be brought about under new dynasties—so long as those who gain power remain faithful to God, which in human societies is never the case. There is therefore a continuing need for prophecy, so that God's voice may be heard—and heeded—in the world today.

Elijah was not merely a prophet of a particular form of religious orthodoxy, opposed to the worship of other gods, nor even of social justice and the rights of the weak and vulnerable. While these are important aspects of Elijah's pronouncements, they do not encapsulate either God's essence or God's message. Elijah's is one of the earliest testimonies we have to the recognition that God's purposes extend beyond the narrow, nationalistic, and often chauvinist and xenophobic interests of Israel. Not only did Elijah instigate revolution in Syria, but his ministry testifies to ways in which people of other nations may demonstrate faith in God and play a part in the fulfilment of God's purposes. Two incidents recorded during a period of famine, brought about through the drought Elijah had pronounced as a sign of God's judgement on Israel, illustrate this.

Elijah takes refuge in the region of Zarephath, a Phoenician city on the coast of what is now Lebanon:

> Then the word of the Lord came to him, saying, "Go now to Zarephath, which belongs to Sidon, and live there; for I have commanded a widow there to feed you." So he set out and went to Zarephath. When he came to the gate of the town, a widow was there gathering sticks; he called to her and said, "Bring me a little water in a vessel, so that I may drink." As she was going to bring it, he called to her and said, "Bring me a morsel of bread in your hand." But she said, "As the Lord your God lives, I have nothing baked, only a handful of meal in a jar, and a little oil

in a jug; I am now gathering a couple of sticks, so that I may go home and prepare it for myself and my son, that we may eat it, and die." Elijah said to her, "Do not be afraid; go and do as you have said; but first make me a little cake of it and bring it to me, and afterwards make something for yourself and your son. For thus says the Lord the God of Israel: The jar of meal will not be emptied and the jug of oil will not fail until the day that the Lord sends rain on the earth." She went and did as Elijah said, so that she as well as he and her household ate for many days. The jar of meal was not emptied, neither did the jug of oil fail, according to the word of the Lord that he spoke by Elijah (1 Kings 17:8-16).

The widow, who is never named or otherwise identified, recognizes Elijah as a prophet of a god whom she did not otherwise know or worship. Furthermore, she responds in faith to his request for food—one which she might quite justifiably have looked upon as grossly unreasonable in the circumstances. While we are not told the circumstances of her husband's death, there is no suggestion that his family in any way cared for her, and we are left with the impression that her son was a child entirely dependent on her care. The widow was therefore in a particularly vulnerable position, quite possibly living in poverty even before the famine. Yet in giving Elijah of the last of the food which stood between her and her son's death by starvation, the widow made possible not only the survival of all three, but the continuation of God's prophetic word through Elijah. Her faith was to be tested further:

> After this the son of the woman, the mistress of the house, became ill; his illness was so severe that there was no breath left in him. She then said to Elijah, "What have you against me, O man of God? You have come to me to bring my sin to remembrance, and to cause the death of my son!" But he said to her, "Give me your son." He took him from her bosom, carried him up into the upper chamber where he was lodging, and laid him on his own bed. He cried out to the Lord, "O Lord my God, have you brought calamity even upon the widow with whom I am staying, by killing her son?" Then he stretched himself upon the child three times, and cried out to the Lord, "O Lord my God, let this child's life come into him again." The Lord listened to the voice of Elijah; the life of the child came into him again, and he revived. Elijah took the child, brought him down from the upper chamber into the house, and gave him to his mother; then Elijah said, "See, your son is alive." So the woman said to Elijah, "Now I know that you are a man of God, and that the word of the Lord in your mouth is truth" (1 Kings 17:17-24).

The death of the boy tested the faith not only of his mother, but of Elijah himself. God's mercy in reviving the child confirms his mother's faith, acknowledging not only the supernatural power manifested in Elijah, but his standing as the prophet of God who had hitherto been unknown and alien to her.

This story is preceded by another intriguing episode:

> Now Elijah the Tishbite, of Tishbe in Gilead, said to Ahab, "As the Lord the God of Israel lives, before whom I stand, there shall be neither dew nor rain these years, except by my word." The word of the Lord came to him, saying, "Go from here and turn eastwards, and hide yourself by the Wadi Cherith, which is east of the Jordan. You shall drink from the wadi, and I have commanded the ravens to feed you there." So he went and did according to the word of the Lord; he went and lived by the Wadi Cherith, which is east of the Jordan. The ravens brought him bread and meat in the morning, and bread and meat in the evening; and he drank from the wadi. But after a while the wadi dried up, because there was no rain in the land (1 Kings 17:1-7).

On any reading, this episode would be discomforting to an observant Jew, scrupulous in observance of the purity laws. Ravens are described as "detestable" and "an abomination" in the Law of Moses, and eating their meat is absolutely prohibited (Leviticus 11:13-19; Deuteronomy 14:14). These are not merely strong expressions for "disgusting", but the visceral repugnance at birds which eat carrion reflects association with evil (Deuteronomy 14:21). The raven released from the ark by Noah (Genesis 8:6-7), which, unlike the dove, did not return with a symbol of life and hope, is the first named bird in Scripture. Rabbinic tradition interprets this episode as expulsion from the ark for copulating during the flood and explains that the raven did not return as it was feeding off the corpses of people who had drowned in the flood. Readers and hearers of this story might well have wondered what kind of meat the ravens brought Elijah. While part of God's creation, and beneficiaries of God's gracious provision for all creatures (Job 38:41; Psalm 147:9; cf. Luke 12:24), ravens were nonetheless repulsive, and to eat food which they had provided would have involved transgression of purity laws. However dire the circumstances, this is significant.

Another interpretation of this episode is possible. The Hebrew word '*rbym* usually rendered "ravens" could also be rendered "Arabs".[5] If Arabs came to Wadi Cherith, at

---

[5] The Hebrew alphabet consists only of consonants, and the same set of (usually three or occasionally four) consonants could spell quite different words, pronounced differently according to their associated vowels. Marks, known as diacritics, to indicate vowel sounds were introduced to Hebrew texts during the medieval period. The consonants '*rbym* could be vocalized either as '*orbim* (ravens) or as '*arabim* (Arabs).

God's command, to feed Elijah, this would be another example of people of other nations demonstrating righteousness and kindness to God's prophet. Not only would they so enable the prophet to persevere in his work, but they themselves would become part of that work. While this is a minority reading of the text, it would be consistent with the much longer pericope which follows.

However tenuous his connection with Bethlehem, Elijah is significant for our Advent observance. Not only does he pronounce God's judgement, at considerable cost to himself, but he includes people of other nations in the work God is doing in and through Israel. In this, he precedes Isaiah and other later prophets in preparing for the coming of the One who would be the light to the gentiles.

Questions for discussion

1. It was noted that Elijah is commemorated at Bethlehem, but there is no historical evidence that he ever visited the area. How important is this for his significance for Advent, and for the enduring significance of his testimony?
2. God's judgement pronounced by Elijah resulted in hunger and thirst not only in Israel but in neighbouring lands, and the rulers of Israel whose idolatry incurred God's wrath would have been

among those who suffered least. What does this say about the ways in which we see suffering in the world around us? How do we discern God's work and God's judgement in the world today?
3. Elijah instigated the violent overthrow of the kings of Israel and Syria. What does this say about Christian attitudes to political rulers and other authority figures in the world today?
4. When Elijah was a fugitive, he found shelter and sustenance from foreigners, who provided for him at great risk to themselves. What does this say about our attitude to refugees? What does it say about our willingness to discern God at work in strangers?

Points for prayer

1. All who suffer as a consequence of rulers and other people's abuses of power and of God's creation.
2. All who give of the little they have to relieve the suffering of others.
3. All who have been forced to flee their homes to seek shelter among strangers.
4. All who are forcibly separated from places they hold sacred, and where they have experienced God's presence.

The traditional site of Jesus' birth, in the Grotto of the Nativity, beneath the sanctuary of the Church of the Nativity, Bethlehem. Photograph by the author, 2015

5

Jesus

The Christian New Testament includes four Gospels, of which two include an account of the birth of Jesus. It is worth reminding ourselves that the narrative of the Gospel of Mark opens with Jesus as an adult, coming to the Jordan to be baptized by the prophet John, known to us as John the Baptist or John the Baptizer:

> The beginning of the good news of Jesus Christ, the Son of God.
>
> As it is written in the prophet Isaiah, "See, I am sending my messenger ahead of you, who will prepare your way; the voice of one crying out in the wilderness: 'Prepare the way of the Lord, make his paths straight'", John the baptizer appeared in the wilderness, proclaiming a baptism of repentance for the forgiveness of sins. And people from the whole Judean countryside and all the people of Jerusalem were going out to him, and were baptized by him in the river Jordan, confessing their sins. Now John was clothed with camel's hair, with a leather belt around his waist, and he ate locusts and wild

> honey. He proclaimed, "The one who is more powerful than I is coming after me; I am not worthy to stoop down and untie the thong of his sandals. I have baptized you with water; but he will baptize you with the Holy Spirit."
>
> In those days Jesus came from Nazareth of Galilee and was baptized by John in the Jordan. And just as he was coming up out of the water, he saw the heavens torn apart and the Spirit descending like a dove on him. And a voice came from heaven, "You are my Son, the Beloved; with you I am well pleased" (Mark 1:1-11).

The Gospel of John opens with a Prologue expounding upon the eternal *Logos*, or Word of God, who became incarnate in Jesus of Nazareth:

> In the beginning was the Word, and the Word was with God, and the Word was God. He was in the beginning with God. All things came into being through him, and without him not one thing came into being. What has come into being in him was life, and the life was the light of all people. The light shines in the darkness, and the darkness did not overcome it.
>
> There was a man sent from God, whose name was John. He came as a witness to testify to the light, so that all might believe through him. He

himself was not the light, but he came to testify to the light. The true light, which enlightens everyone, was coming into the world.

He was in the world, and the world came into being through him; yet the world did not know him. He came to what was his own, and his own people did not accept him. But to all who received him, who believed in his name, he gave power to become children of God, who were born, not of blood or of the will of the flesh or of the will of man, but of God.

And the Word became flesh and lived among us, and we have seen his glory, the glory as of a father's only son, full of grace and truth (John 1:1-14).

It is in the Gospels of Matthew and Luke that we read of Jesus' birth in Bethlehem. Each tells the story quite differently, and our understanding of Jesus' birth would be very different if only one of these Gospels had come down to us. While the conflation and imaginative embellishment of the two stories has been part of Christian memory since at least the second century, and continues in the nativity plays we enjoy in schools and churches today, it may be instructive to pause, and reflect on what we might learn, what we might see differently, if we had only one of the Gospel nativity narratives.

The site identified by tradition, at least as old as the third or early fourth century, as the place of Jesus' birth, is the focal point around which Bethlehem was rebuilt under the patronage of the empress Helena. The city has grown over the centuries, attracting pilgrims from all over the Christian world, and also monks and nuns who have formed communities around Bethlehem, providing hospitality to pilgrims, education and healthcare to the local community, and continuous prayer, witness and worship in a place sanctified by the memory of Jesus' birth, of God's coming into the world in a unique and saving way.

The birth of Jesus is sacred to Muslims as well as to Christians. The Qur'an preserves an account of the Annunciation:

> The angels said to Mary: "Mary, God has chosen you and made you pure: He has truly chosen you above all women. Mary, be devout to your Lord, prostrate yourself in worship, bow down with those who pray." This is an account of things beyond your knowledge that We reveal to you [Muhammad]: you were not present among them when they cast lots to see which of them should take charge of Mary, you were not present with them when they argued [about her]. The angels said, "Mary, God gives you news of a Word from Him, whose name will be the Messiah, Jesus, son of Mary, who will be

held in honour in this world and the next, who will be one of those brought near to God. He will speak to people in his infancy and in his adulthood. He will be one of the righteous." She said, "My Lord, how can I have a son when no man has touched me?" [The angel] said, "This is how God creates what He will: when He has ordained something. He only says, 'Be', and it is. He will teach him the Scripture and wisdom, the Torah and the Gospel, He will send him as a messenger to the Children of Israel" (*Qur'an* 3, *Al 'Imram* 42-9).

It preserves also an account of Mary's pregnancy and Jesus' birth:

> Mention in the Qur'an the story of Mary. She withdrew from her family to a place to the east and secluded herself away; We sent Our Spirit to appear before her in the form of a perfected man. She said, "I seek the Lord of Mercy's protection against you: if you have any fear of Him [do not approach]!" but he said, "I am but a Messenger from your Lord, [come] to announce to you the gift of a pure son." She said, "How can I have a son when no man has touched me? I have not been unchaste," and he said, "This is what your Lord said: 'It is easy for Me—We shall make him a sign to all people, a blessing from Us.'"

And so it was ordained: she conceived him. She withdrew to a distant place and, when the pains of childbirth drove her to [cling to] the trunk of a palm tree, she exclaimed, "I wish I had been dead and forgotten long before all this!" but a voice cried to her from below, "Do not worry: your Lord has provided a stream at your feet and, if you shake the trunk of the palm tree towards you, it will deliver fresh ripe dates for you, so eat, drink, be glad, and say to anyone you may see: 'I have vowed to the Lord of Mercy to abstain from conversation, and I will not talk to anyone today.'"

She went back to her people carrying the child, and they said, "Mary! You have done something terrible! Sister of Aaron! Your father was not an evil man; your mother was not unchaste!" She pointed at him. They said, "How can we converse with an infant?" [But] he said: "I am a servant of God. He has granted me the Scripture; made me a prophet; made me blessed wherever I may be. He commanded me to pray, to give alms as long as I live, to cherish my mother. He did not make me domineering or graceless. Peace was on me the day I was born, and will be on me the day I die and the day I am raised to life again." Such was Jesus, son of Mary.

[This is] a statement of the Truth about which they are in doubt: it would not befit God to have a child. He is far above that: when He decrees something, He says only, "Be," and it is. "God is my Lord and your Lord, so serve Him: that is a straight path" (*Qur'an* 19, *Maryam* 16-36).

It is worth noting that Muslim tradition conflates Mary, the mother of Jesus, with Miriam, the sister of Moses and Aaron, the versions of their names by which they are known in Christian Scripture deriving from the same Hebrew root. In the biblical narrative, the two are separated by well over a millennium, but it is not uncommon in ancient oral traditions for people of the same name to be associated or identified. Early Christian traditions identify Zechariah, the father of John the Baptist, with the prophet of the same name, and also with the high priest murdered in the temple by King Joash (2 Chronicles 24:21; cf. Matthew 23:35; Luke 11:50-1).

As well as cherishing the story of Jesus' birth, Muslims pray at the place associated with the birth of him who is one of the greatest of their prophets. They too revere Mary, or Maryam, the mother of Jesus who not merely has a *sura* of the Qur'an named after her, but is one of the most frequently mentioned characters in the sacred text of Islam; Moses (Musa), Jesus (Issa) and Abraham (Ibrahim) being the most frequently named.

For Jews, the position of Jesus is very much more difficult, largely on account of the long history of persecution which the Jewish people have suffered, especially but not only in Christian Europe. Jesus was born a Jew, we need all to remember, and while the place associated with his birth has never been, and is unlikely to become, a place of Jewish pilgrimage, many Jewish scholars are finding in Jesus, or *Yeshua* as he is known in modern Hebrew, an important and neglected teacher of their faith—and for some the greatest. While Messianic Judaism[1] is a diverse and growing movement, and Hebrew Catholic[2] congregations are maintaining and developing their distinctive character under the auspices of the Latin Patriarchate of Jerusalem, it remains the case that most Jews are not able to accept Jesus as the Messiah in the way that Christians have come to understand him. It is nevertheless important that we appreciate that Jesus is a significant figure for Jews and Muslims, as well as for Christians.

In the Gospel of Luke, the nativity story begins not in Bethlehem, but in the temple in Jerusalem, and with the account of the birth, not of Jesus but of John the Baptist. It is only in Luke that we are told that John was born into the priesthood, which in Israel is hereditary, and that through his mother Elizabeth he is related to Jesus.

---

[1] Messianic Judaism refers to a number of Jewish movements which acknowledge Jesus of Nazareth as the Messiah, but continue to live and worship as Jews, in their own communities, and do not join gentile Christian denominations.

[2] Hebrew Catholic communities include both Jews who have converted to Roman Catholic Christianity and (gentile) migrant workers in Israel. They worship in Hebrew, and some Jewish customs have been incorporated in their liturgies.

Mary enters the story in Nazareth, a town in Galilee far to the north of Bethlehem. As a young girl, betrothed but not yet married, she learns, through the angel Gabriel, that she has been chosen to be the mother of God's son. In agrarian societies of this period, girls tended to be married very young, often to much older men, and with or without their consent. Mary, perhaps no more than 12 or 13 years old, submits to the will of God, and accepts her calling to be the mother of God's son, despite the perils of pregnancy. For a woman or girl not yet married to become pregnant was shameful, and brought dishonour on her family, for which the penalty could have been what has come to be known as "honour killing". Jesus is conceived, not through sexual union but through the working of God's Spirit, and in the face of social ostracism and the risk of murder.

It is the requirement of the imperial rulers that Joseph, a descendant of David, present himself in his hometown for census registration, that takes Mary at an advanced stage in her pregnancy to Bethlehem, where Jesus is born. It is difficult for us to appreciate the perils of travel in the ancient world, and just how vulnerable a pregnant woman would have been to the hazards which confronted travellers. Quite apart from the dangers posed by bandits, and the stress and exhaustion of enforced travel—by foot on poor and uneven roads—Mary would have been separated from her family, the people on whose support she would normally have counted in the days before childbirth became hospitalized and support professionalized. Instead of the comfort, or at least the familiarity, of her home, Mary gave birth in crowded and insanitary conditions because the inn was filled to overflowing.

The first visitors to the infant Jesus, and the first to offer him worship, are shepherds, to whom angels disclose what has taken place while they are guarding their flocks through the night. It is easy to be sentimental about the scene, as it is about the stable and the manger, but it is important to recognize that shepherds' work was dangerous, as they and their sheep were vulnerable to predatory animals and to bandits. As people who needed to spend nights away from their homes and families, shepherds were looked upon as morally suspect by many who enjoyed a more privileged and more secure position in society. David may have been born into a prominent family, but he was the youngest of eight sons, and therefore was not deemed of sufficient honour to be invited to the feast until Samuel insisted he be summoned (1 Samuel 16:11-12). Yet not only were despised shepherds chosen to receive the news of Jesus' birth, but he was later to model his ministry on that of the Good Shepherd:

> "Very truly, I tell you, anyone who does not enter the sheepfold by the gate but climbs in by another way is a thief and a bandit. The one who enters by the gate is the shepherd of the sheep. The gatekeeper opens the gate for him, and the

sheep hear his voice. He calls his own sheep by name and leads them out. When he has brought out all his own, he goes ahead of them, and the sheep follow him because they know his voice. They will not follow a stranger, but they will run from him because they do not know the voice of strangers". Jesus used this figure of speech with them, but they did not understand what he was saying to them. So again Jesus said to them, "Very truly, I tell you, I am the gate for the sheep. All who came before me are thieves and bandits; but the sheep did not listen to them. I am the gate. Whoever enters by me will be saved, and will come in and go out and find pasture. The thief comes only to steal and kill and destroy. I came that they may have life, and have it abundantly. I am the good shepherd. The good shepherd lays down his life for the sheep. The hired hand, who is not the shepherd and does not own the sheep, sees the wolf coming and leaves the sheep and runs away—and the wolf snatches them and scatters them. The hired hand runs away because a hired hand does not care for the sheep. I am the good shepherd. I know my own and my own know me, just as the Father knows me and I know the Father. And I lay down my life for the sheep. I have other sheep that do not belong to this fold. I must bring them also, and they will listen to my voice. So there will be one flock, one shepherd. For this reason the Father loves me, because I lay down my life in order to take it up again. No one takes it from me, but I lay it down of my own accord. I have power to lay it down, and I have power to take it up again. I have received this command from my Father" (John 10:1-18).

The psalm, traditionally attributed to David, the shepherd who became king, uses the shepherd as an image of God:

> The Lord is my shepherd, I shall not want.
> > He makes me lie down in green pastures;
> he leads me beside still waters;
> > he restores my soul.
> He leads me in right paths
> > for his name's sake.
> Even though I walk through the
> > darkest valley, I fear no evil;
> for you are with me; your rod and
> > your staff—they comfort me.
> You prepare a table before me in the
> > presence of my enemies;
> you anoint my head with oil; my cup overflows.
> Surely goodness and mercy shall follow
> > me all the days of my life,
> and I shall dwell in the house of the Lord
> > my whole life long (Psalm 23).

God chooses those who are common and often despised, and the work they do, as one of the most vivid models of Jesus' ministry.

The traditional location of the angels' visit to the shepherds is in Beit Sahour. Much of the fields have been built over, to accommodate refugees from other parts of Palestine as well as the natural growth of Bethlehem. Beneath the modern church, built on the site of a fifth-century chapel marking the site, is a cave, now furnished as a chapel, which is believed to have been used as a place of shelter for sheep and shepherds at the time of Jesus' birth.

The Gospel of Matthew gives a rather different account of the birth of Jesus:

> Now the birth of Jesus the Messiah took place in this way. When his mother Mary had been engaged to Joseph, but before they lived together, she was found to be with child from the Holy Spirit. Her husband Joseph, being a righteous man and unwilling to expose her to public disgrace, planned to dismiss her quietly. But just when he had resolved to do this, an angel of the Lord appeared to him in a dream and said, "Joseph, son of David, do not be afraid to take Mary as your wife, for the child conceived in her is from the Holy Spirit. She will bear a son, and you are to name him Jesus, for he will save his people from their sins." All this

took place to fulfil what had been spoken by the Lord through the prophet:

"Look, the virgin shall conceive and bear a son, and they shall name him Emmanuel", which means, "God is with us."

When Joseph awoke from sleep, he did as the angel of the Lord commanded him; he took her as his wife, but had no marital relations with her until she had borne a son; and he named him Jesus (Matthew 1:18-25).

Joseph's descent from the royal line of David is emphasized, and there is no indication that his home, or that of Mary his betrothed, is anywhere other than Bethlehem. When Joseph discovers that Mary is pregnant before they are married, he decides to terminate the betrothal discreetly. Rather than publicly shaming Mary, and leaving her vulnerable to the arbitrary justice which might be meted out by elders of the community, or what today might be termed "honour killing", Joseph decides to release Mary from her obligations to him, so that she could marry the father and they could raise their child together. Joseph must presumably have believed that there was another man, and that Mary's pregnancy implied an emotional as well as physical intimacy he did not enjoy with her; he therefore frees her to marry the man of her choice. If Mary had been violated, there would have been no such man, and Mary would have been left vulnerable, not so much as a single parent raising a child alone, as the likely victim of the "justice" meted out in local communities.

The assurances of the angel, received in a dream, persuade Joseph to proceed with his marriage to Mary, accepting the child to be born as the fruit of God's intervention.

In the Old Testament, God had intervened in the conception of Isaac, in the episode of Abraham's hospitality to strangers which the Church has long interpreted as a type of the Trinity:

> The Lord appeared to Abraham by the oaks of Mamre, as he sat at the entrance of his tent in the heat of the day. He looked up and saw three men standing near him. When he saw them, he ran from the tent entrance to meet them, and bowed down to the ground. He said, "My lord, if I find favour with you, do not pass by your servant. Let a little water be brought, and wash your feet, and rest yourselves under the tree. Let me bring a little bread, that you may refresh yourselves, and after that you may pass on—since you have come to your servant." So they said, "Do as you have said." And Abraham hastened into the tent to Sarah, and said, "Make ready quickly three measures of choice flour, knead it, and make cakes." Abraham ran to the

herd, and took a calf, tender and good, and gave it to the servant, who hastened to prepare it. Then he took curds and milk and the calf that he had prepared, and set it before them; and he stood by them under the tree while they ate. They said to him, "Where is your wife Sarah?" And he said, "There, in the tent." Then one said, "I will surely return to you in due season, and your wife Sarah shall have a son." And Sarah was listening at the tent entrance behind him. Now Abraham and Sarah were old, advanced in age; it had ceased to be with Sarah after the manner of women. So Sarah laughed to herself, saying, "After I have grown old, and my husband is old, shall I have pleasure?" The Lord said to Abraham, "Why did Sarah laugh, and say, 'Shall I indeed bear a child, now that I am old?' Is anything too wonderful for the Lord? At the set time I will return to you, in due season, and Sarah shall have a son." But Sarah denied, saying, "I did not laugh"; for she was afraid. He said, "Oh yes, you did laugh" (Genesis 18:1-15).

God's intervention in the birth of Samuel causes his mother, Hannah, to express her praise to God in words which evoke those of Mary in Luke 1:

> After they had eaten and drunk at Shiloh, Hannah rose and presented herself before the

Lord. Now Eli the priest was sitting on the seat beside the doorpost of the temple of the Lord. She was deeply distressed and prayed to the Lord, and wept bitterly. She made this vow: "O Lord of hosts, if only you will look on the misery of your servant, and remember me, and not forget your servant, but will give to your servant a male child, then I will set him before you as a nazirite until the day of his death. He shall drink neither wine nor intoxicants, and no razor shall touch his head." As she continued praying before the Lord, Eli observed her mouth. Hannah was praying silently; only her lips moved, but her voice was not heard; therefore Eli thought she was drunk. So Eli said to her, "How long will you make a drunken spectacle of yourself? Put away your wine." But Hannah answered, "No, my lord, I am a woman deeply troubled; I have drunk neither wine nor strong drink, but I have been pouring out my soul before the Lord. Do not regard your servant as a worthless woman, for I have been speaking out of my great anxiety and vexation all this time." Then Eli answered, "Go in peace; the God of Israel grant the petition you have made to him." And she said, "Let your servant find favour in your sight." Then the woman went to her quarters, ate and drank with her husband, and her countenance was sad no longer (1 Samuel 1:9-18).

In these and other cases in the Old Testament, God's intervention is to bless the union of husband and wife so that pregnancy and childbirth would follow. Similarly with the birth of John the Baptist in Luke 1. But, in the case of Jesus, no human father is identified, and Joseph is directed to receive and to raise as his own the child conceived in Mary through the intervention of God's Spirit.

The birth of Jesus comes to the attention of King Herod, who ruled Judaea as a vassal of the Romans:

> In the time of King Herod, after Jesus was born in Bethlehem of Judea, wise men from the East came to Jerusalem, asking, "Where is the child who has been born king of the Jews? For we observed his star at its rising, and have come to pay him homage." When King Herod heard this, he was frightened, and all Jerusalem with him; and calling together all the chief priests and scribes of the people, he inquired of them where the Messiah was to be born. They told him, 'In Bethlehem of Judea; for so it has been written by the prophet:
>
> "And you, Bethlehem, in the land of Judah,
>   are by no means least among the rulers of Judah;
> for from you shall come a ruler
>   who is to shepherd my people Israel"
>   (Matthew 2:1-6).

The palace is alerted through the visit of the "wise men", often known as the Magi, from the Greek word *magoi*. *Magoi* can be translated in a number of ways, of which "wise men" is one of the more polite possibilities: this is the word from which "magic" and "magician" derive. They are presumably not Jews, or even necessarily worshippers of the God of Israel, but their identity and origins are not disclosed. The term *magoi* may designate Zoroastrian priests, or members of a particular Medo-Persian tribe, living in what is now Iran, but more often refers to sophists and practitioners of augury, oneiromancy (interpretation of dreams), or astrology—the skill in which these particular Magi are versed. While modern minds may draw a clear distinction between astrology and astronomy, and tend to disparage the former, the ancient world knew no such distinction.

The Magi would therefore be perceived as possessing great skill, knowledge and wisdom. The science of the heavenly bodies nonetheless falls short of insights gained through meditation on Scripture. The work of God, revealed in creation and interpreted in Scripture, is the basis of Jewish wisdom. Matthew does not mention how many Magi there were, nor indeed that they were male. Nor does he identify them as kings—that is a second-century development in the tradition; it is not their status, but the rumour circulating on account of their presence in the city, which brings them to the attention of the court. Furthermore, their wisdom is somewhat ambiguous, as demonstrated in their arriving in Jerusalem and Herod's palace while supposedly following the star to Bethlehem.

While the status of the Magi is not as eminent as later tradition has accorded them, their interaction with Herod's court brings the infant Jesus into peril. While a powerful and at times brutal ruler, the ageing Herod enjoyed little legitimacy in the eyes of most Jews. The prospect of a rival emerging in what would have been the closing years of his long reign, particularly a king from the family of David, would have galvanized the court and its extensive security apparatus. Herod deceives the Magi as to his intentions—another indication that they may not have been so wise after all, when continuing their quest for the infant king imperilled him whom they had come to worship.

The homage, and gifts of gold, frankincense and myrrh, offered to Jesus have, by tradition, served to identify the Magi as the first gentiles to worship Christ. While it would be more than an exaggeration to identify them as representing the pinnacle of pagan wisdom, it is nonetheless significant that, in this most Jewish of Gospels, the first worship offered to the king of the Jews is brought by gentiles, almost certainly not worshippers of the God of Israel. These evade Herod's court on their return journey, and are never mentioned again in the Gospel. Meanwhile:

When Herod saw that he had been tricked by the wise men, he was infuriated, and he sent and killed all the children in and around Bethlehem who were two years old or under, according to the time that he had learned from the wise men. Then was fulfilled what had been spoken through the prophet Jeremiah:

'A voice was heard in Ramah,
  wailing and loud lamentation,
Rachel weeping for her children;
  she refused to be consoled,
  because they are no more' (Matthew 2:16-18).

The slaughter of the children of Bethlehem ordered by Herod was not at all out of character with the brutality of his reign; Josephus records several other incidents. The sanctification by the later Church of the "Holy Innocents" as the first martyrs must not obscure the shock and horror of this atrocity. Irrespective of the number of children killed, this is what today would be called a crime against humanity.

Joseph evades Herod's massacre by fleeing Bethlehem and taking his wife and child to Egypt:

> Now after they had left, an angel of the Lord appeared to Joseph in a dream and said, "Get up, take the child and his mother, and flee to Egypt, and remain there until I tell you; for

> Herod is about to search for the child, to destroy him." Then Joseph got up, took the child and his mother by night, and went to Egypt, and remained there until the death of Herod. This was to fulfil what had been spoken by the Lord through the prophet, "Out of Egypt I have called my son" (Matthew 2:13-15).

To the south of the Church of the Nativity stands the Milk Grotto, identified since the fourth century as a place in which the Holy Family found refuge. The site is sacred to both Christians and Muslims, and especially to new mothers and to women wishing to conceive. The name derives from a tradition that the white chalk of the cave derives its colour from Mary's having spilt a drop of milk while nursing Jesus.

The flight into Egypt would have been long and perilous, especially for a young baby and his mother, recovering from the strains of pregnancy and childbirth. It is estimated that the journey from Bethlehem to Pelusium, the Egyptian city closest to the border with Judaea, would have taken about 30 days. The roads were infested with bandits, and obtaining food and shelter along the route would have been uncertain. Their journey would almost certainly have taken them through Gaza, now home to over a million refugees and their descendants; people who lost homes and land during the *Nakba*, and after the 1967 war, and who have been losing their homes again during the current onslaught of the Israeli armed forces. About seventeen thousand children have been killed during the latest, and most vicious, Israeli bombing campaign on Gaza.[3] It is small wonder that charges of genocide have been laid against Israel before the International Court of Justice, and that the atrocities have evoked memories of the murder of the children of Bethlehem by Herod.

When they finally passed from Herod's territories into Egypt, Joseph and Mary may have been relieved of their fear of pursuit, but being able to find a home and livelihood in a place of exile would have depended on the goodwill of strangers. Jewish communities had been settled in parts of Egypt for centuries, and it would have been among these that the family would have sought shelter. Anti-Jewish riots are known to have taken place in Egypt from time to time, and Herod's agents would have been able to penetrate Jewish communities in diaspora, so even in exile their safety would have been far from certain. Matthew passes over this period in silence, but the Coptic Orthodox Church in Egypt preserves and cherishes traditions of the sojourn of the Holy Family in that land. Some of these continue to be commemorated at associated sites of pilgrimage today. It is important for us all to remember that Jesus began life as a refugee, and that life in exile would have been far from secure for his family.

---

[3] Statistics are extremely difficult to verify, and are constantly increasing, in the prevailing circumstances. The figure cited derives from reliable sources, and is probably a conservative estimate.

Matthew recounts that, on hearing of Herod's death, Joseph took his family back to Judaea but, not wishing to live in the territory of Herod's son Archelaus, moved north to Nazareth in Galilee, an area ruled by another of Herod's sons, Antipas—the tetrarch remembered for having John the Baptist imprisoned and then executed, and who appears also in Luke's account of Jesus' trial.

A major theme in Matthew's account of the birth of Jesus is demonstrating how the events recorded in the Gospel bring to fulfilment prophecies found in Scripture, in the books which Christians call the Old Testament:

> A star shall come out of Jacob, and a sceptre shall rise out of Israel (Numbers 24:17).

> Therefore the Lord himself will give you a sign. Look, the young woman is with child and shall bear a son, and shall name him Immanuel (Isaiah 7:14).

> A shoot shall come out from the stock of Jesse, and a branch shall grow out of his roots (Isaiah 11:1).

> The days are surely coming, says the Lord, when I will raise up for David a righteous Branch, and he shall reign as king and deal wisely, and shall

> execute justice and righteousness in the land (Jeremiah 23:5).

> A voice is heard in Ramah, lamentation and bitter weeping. Rachel is weeping for her children; she refuses to be comforted for her children, because they are no more (Jeremiah 31:15).

> When Israel was a child, I loved him, and out of Egypt I called my son (Hosea 11:1).

Passages which had hitherto been understood quite differently, and are still understood quite differently by Jewish readers for whom these books remain sacred Scripture, are re-interpreted in the light of the Christian experience of Jesus. For Christians, Jesus both transforms and fulfils the hopes of Israel, as expressed in the sacred texts. This reflects two thousand years of reflection by the followers of Jesus, who from the earliest times turned to Scripture to discern the meaning and significance of what they had experienced of God's work in the world in the person of Jesus. These texts are an example of this, and the same process permeates the letters of the apostle Paul. And, in the Gospels, Jesus speaks of fulfilment, not least in his identification of John the Baptist with Elijah. But, for Jews who do not share in the Christian experience of God in Jesus Christ, it would be quite impossible to discern fulfilment of prophecy in his life, death and resurrection, and still less in the proclamation of the gospel by the Christian Church.

The Gospels, and other early Christian writings, identify Jesus as a descendant of David:

> An account of the genealogy of Jesus the Messiah, the son of David, the son of Abraham (Matthew 1:1).

> When he heard that it was Jesus of Nazareth, he began to shout out and say, "Jesus, Son of David, have mercy on me!" Many sternly ordered him to be quiet, but he cried out even more loudly, "Son of David, have mercy on me!" (Mark 10:47-8).

> "Blessed is the coming kingdom of our ancestor David! Hosanna in the highest heaven!" (Mark 11:10).

> While Jesus was teaching in the temple, he said, "How can the scribes say that the Messiah is the son of David? David himself, by the Holy Spirit, declared, 'The Lord said to my Lord, "Sit at my right hand, until I put your enemies under your feet."' David himself calls him Lord; so how can he be his son?" And the large crowd was listening to him with delight (Mark 12:35-7).

> Paul, a servant of Jesus Christ, called to be an apostle, set apart for the gospel of God, which he promised beforehand through his prophets in the holy scriptures, the gospel concerning his Son, who was descended from David according to the flesh and was declared to be Son of God with power according to the spirit of holiness by resurrection from the dead, Jesus Christ our Lord, through whom we have received grace and apostleship to bring about the obedience of faith among all the Gentiles for the sake of his name, including yourselves who are called to belong to Jesus Christ (Romans 1:1-6).

> Then one of the elders said to me, "Do not weep. See, the Lion of the tribe of Judah, the Root of David, has conquered, so that he can open the scroll and its seven seals" (Revelation 5:5).

These passages all claim for Jesus the status of heir to a throne long vacant. The same texts are equally clear that Jesus is quite unlike David in the nature of his rule.

Whatever the Roman rulers may have suspected when they crucified him, Jesus did not aspire to establish an earthly kingdom, and his disciples were not a military unit of any kind. Whereas David appears a bandit, or what today might be called a warlord, before he becomes king, Jesus proclaims the coming of God's kingdom, teaches the people to live according to its ethics, heals the sick, exorcises those suffering possession, and trains his disciples to continue his work. Jesus brings to fulfilment God's promises, not by means of earthly power or attempts to seize such power, but by proclaiming and witnessing to God's rule through his life, and through his death and resurrection.

Questions for discussion

1. Matthew and Luke tell the story of Jesus' birth in different ways. What can be learned from reading the account in one of these Gospels without reference to the other, or to the tradition which has coalesced and embellished these stories?
2. In the Gospel accounts of Jesus' birth in both Matthew and Luke, Mary faces the prospect of becoming a single parent. If Joseph had repudiated her, she would have been vulnerable not merely to the perils of pregnancy and of raising a child without the support of a husband and extended family, but also to judgement and ostracism by her community. She would have been liable to "honour killing" for bringing shame on her family. What do these risks teach us about the cost of obeying God, of accepting that our calling may not be merely inconvenient but perilous?
3. The shepherds in Luke are, on account of the nature of their work and their marginal and

vulnerable position in society, despised and morally suspect members of the community in the eyes of the privileged and powerful. Yet they are chosen to be the first to receive the news of Christ's birth, and the first to worship him. What does this teach us about our mission as a church?

4. The Magi in Matthew are outsiders to the Covenant. Their quest for the infant king of the Jews brings them to Jesus, but their knowledge is founded on science rather than reflection on the Hebrew Scriptures. What does this teach us about those who find their way into our churches, uncertain of what they are seeking? What does it teach about attitudes to people of other faiths or none, and their quest for God? What does it teach us about how we are to receive those who enter our places of worship and seek our fellowship, but are not obviously "one of us"?

Points for prayer

1. The people of Bethlehem, and Christians around the world, as we come to celebrate God's coming among us in the birth of Jesus.
2. All whose calling in God's service is costly, unconventional or perilous.
3. Women of Bethlehem, and around the world, for whom pregnancy and childbirth incur risks

to their own health and lives, whose access to healthcare is restricted, especially those unable to obtain the help they need on account of the permit system, checkpoints, and the Separation Wall.
4. Women of Bethlehem, and around the world, who are vulnerable to domestic violence; especially those in forced marriages who may be suspected of bringing shame on their families through infidelity, even if they are raped, and the paternity of whose children is doubted; those liable to be victims of "honour killing".
5. Refugees and displaced people, especially those separated from their families and loved ones, and constrained to travel in dangerous conditions; pregnant women and infants who are especially vulnerable to extreme weather, disease, lack of healthcare and sanitation, and to exploitation and violence from people traffickers and from police and armed forces.
6. People traumatized by war, by exile, separation from their families, and by the violent deaths of their children.

Flight into Egypt. Henry Ossawa Tanner, 1916–1922. Public domain.

6

Epiphany Reflection

Epiphany is the Christian festival which commemorates the revelation of God in Christ to the nations. Having observed Advent and celebrated Christmas, our calling is to make Christ known to the world. During Advent, we studied and reflected upon figures from the Old Testament—Rachel, Ruth, David, and Elijah—and on the birth of Jesus. Aspects of these studies may have been as challenging as they were illuminating. We come now to review what we have learned, and to look forward to making this learning part of our Christian lives through the coming year, so that God in Christ may be made known in the world through us.

We read, in the last week, of the Magi, central figures of the Christmas and Epiphany story celebrated in different ways at different times among the diverse Christian traditions which comprise God's Church in Palestine and around the world. The Gospel account does not tell us how many they were or where they came from, notwithstanding later Christian traditions which have numbered them as three, given them the names Melchior, Caspar and Balthazar, and associated them with the continents of Europe, Asia and Africa. Matthew does not identify the Magi as kings, a tradition first attested in writings of the second century. Nor are we told where they went after their visit to Jesus in Bethlehem, other than presumably returning to their homes by a different route (Matthew 2:12). We are not told where this was, or how their visit to Jesus affected the rest of their lives.

The mystery which surrounds the Magi invites us to reflect on ways in which our encounter with Christ affects us. Irrespective of where we have come from—our place of residence, our language and cultural background, our citizenship, our social status, our education, our experience in life—we are confronted with a vulnerable and defenceless infant who is at once like us and at the same time in every way different. Do we simply "go home" and continue our lives as before? Or does our encounter with Jesus mark a significant stage, a turning point, in a journey which continues in different and unexpected directions through the rest of our lives? Whether we undertake a physical or spiritual journey to Bethlehem, by whatever means and following whatever route, where do we go from there?

Returning to our homes, families and work does not mean continuing our lives as before, if we have been changed by our encounter with Jesus. We may not have the gifts of gold, frankincense and myrrh to offer, but

God has given us other gifts—not necessarily to leave behind in Bethlehem, though that too, but to use in God's service wherever our Christian pilgrimage may take us.

Bethlehem, like Jerusalem or Nazareth, or even Medjugorje, Guadaloupe, Lourdes, Compostela or Walsingham, Lindisfarne, Iona, Whithorn or Knock, may be a significant pilgrimage destination, a place where God has been revealed and experienced in particular ways. But the journey does not end there. The return journey may retrace the physical steps of the outward journey, but it is not the same. It is not, or should not be, simply that journey in reverse, but in an important sense an onward journey, to a further destination. As Christians, our ultimate destination is God. Pilgrimage is an opportunity to experience God in new ways, not only by visiting significant places but through encountering other people while doing so— and being changed through that experience, so that as our lives continue, not only are we enriched but we are able to glorify God and proclaim the gospel of Christ in renewed ways.

What has our Advent pilgrimage taught us? How have we experienced God? How have we been changed and enriched? What will be different from now onwards?

Rachel died before reaching the end of her earthly journey, giving birth to Benjamin, the ancestor of Saul, the first king of Israel, and of Saul who became the apostle Paul. What can we learn from her? Jacob's journey continued, and with them God's purposes. Within the purposes of God, Rachel's descendant Saul became king, but he turned from God and his reign ended ignominiously in defeat and death on the battlefield. God's purposes continued with others. The other Saul was a zealous student of *Torah*, God's law contained in Scripture, and he sought its fulfilment in his own day. In doing so he came to persecute the Christian Church—until he encountered God in unexpected ways while on a journey to Damascus. Saul repented, received Baptism, and continued his journey not as an opponent and persecutor but as an apostle of Christ and his gospel. His journey continued to many places where he proclaimed the gospel and established churches, at considerable cost to himself, until Paul glorified God in his death as he had glorified God in his life of arduous work, frequent travel, and intermittent suffering for the gospel of Christ.

Ruth's journey brought her to Bethlehem, where she became part of another family, another nation, an ancestor of David and ultimately of Jesus. She did not return to Moab and all that her background represented. God's purposes were fulfilled in her remaining in the place to which she came. Over the centuries, others have come to Bethlehem and stayed, some pilgrims who have formed communities around the place of Christ's birth, some refugees who have lost their homes and livelihoods and sought shelter where it might be found, struggling to keep alive the hope that one day they will be able to return to the homes from which they were driven, and meanwhile living in the shadow of the shrine which marks the birth of one who left Bethlehem a refugee.

David left Bethlehem to become a soldier, a warlord, and ultimately king of Judah and Israel. His journey brought him hardship and peril before he attained power and wealth. It was precisely when he was secure on the throne that he lost sight of his dependence on God, his regime became exploitative and repressive, and David's sin brought calamity not only on himself but on the people of Israel as a whole. The security derived from earthly power and wealth can be beguiling, corrupting and ultimately destructive. Discipleship is costly and frequently brings suffering and danger, when we need to know our dependence on God, and learn to rely on God rather than our own resources. David was called to repentance by the prophets sent by God. We need to be willing both to heed the words spoken to us in God's name, and also to be willing ourselves to speak the truth in the name of God, challenging those in power, and seeking God's justice in the world.

Elijah passed through Bethlehem as a refugee, seeking food, rest and shelter, before continuing his flight into the wilderness of Sinai. There he met God, but rather than enjoying peace in the divine presence, he was sent back, to stir up revolutions. His mission as God's prophet would not end until he had prepared the way for Elisha to continue his work. Only then would he be released, but the finality or otherwise of his departure remains an enigma, still felt keenly by observant Jews and resolved for Christians in Jesus' identification of John the Baptist as Elijah, who was to come (Matthew 11:14).

Jesus left Bethlehem a child refugee, in peril of his life. The throne he attained was the cross, and thorns his crown. The costly path of suffering, which he experienced as an infant, and consciously followed from his baptism in the Jordan until his crucifixion, brought about God's triumph over evil and death. While God's victory is assured, we are nonetheless called to continue after the example of Christ, playing our part in the completion of his saving work in the world, and accepting our share in the suffering which this entails (Colossians 1:24).

We have, in a sense, visited Bethlehem through our observance of Advent and Christmas, and reflected on people whom God called, who experienced God, and whom God used to fulfil God's purposes in distinctive ways in the world. As we renew our commitment to Christ at Epiphany, a question we need to ask ourselves is: where does our pilgrimage, our discipleship of Christ, take us? Where do we go, and what is God calling us to do?

Notes for Study Leaders

Any course of study is, or should be, an adventure. One which engages with Christian faith embraces a range of intellectual questions and also a deeply human spiritual yearning. These can be challenging to hold together, especially in groups of diverse cultural and educational background, and with different experiences of life in the world. For those in positions of Christian leadership, it can be exciting, but may also feel risky, to encourage a diversity of perceptions to feed, stimulate, challenge and even to provoke each other, and thereby to provide opportunity for all to engage, to think, to pray, and to grow.

There are nevertheless issues which may be very much more complicated, and potentially confusing, for some more than for others, and human responses cannot always be predicted, or attributed entirely to background or education. When it comes to the nature of Scripture, and its authority in our lives, what for some may be an avenue of honest enquiry, or the outcome thereof, may be perceived by others as threatening. While these studies encourage individuals and groups using the material to explore such issues, it will be for leaders to discern how this might most appropriately be done in their pastoral or other contexts, so that people are cared for and affirmed, even as challenging questions are addressed and people may disagree on important issues.

When reading passages from the Bible, for some it may be important to believe that events took place precisely as recounted, involving particular people in particular places at a particular point in human history. For others the same story may relate eternal truths of theological significance, but the historical details are in themselves unimportant. This is very much a "western" problem, as the clear distinction between "truth" and "fiction" or falsehood is a cultural construct rather than being a quality intrinsic to the biblical narratives, or to any other ancient or modern literature. For example, the notion that the world was created in six days, as related in the opening chapter of Genesis, has become a challenge for many western Christians, not because modern sciences have reconstructed very much more complex processes over millions of years from the origins of the universe to the world as we know it, but because modern western minds had been trained to think in terms of truth as scientific fact, without appreciating ways in which truth may be conveyed in other ways in literature, and also in speech—not least in the parables told by Jesus. Nobody has ever been expected to believe that the stories of the "Good Samaritan" or the "Prodigal Son" involved people who actually lived or events which actually took place; nevertheless, those stories convey important truths about God and the world, and are accordingly received by us as part of the gospel. In other words, at least some stories in the Bible convey significant truths which cannot be equated with whether or not the reported events took place at a particular date and time, in a particular place, and involved the particular people named. While the creation narratives in Genesis and the parables of Jesus may seem fairly clear examples of stories which are not conveying historical or scientific facts but expressing theological principles, in many other cases it is far more difficult to ascertain the nature of the truths expressed, and Christians may honestly and openly disagree on such matters.

In order to assist leaders to prepare and manage constructive discussions, some information will be provided concerning the nature of the biblical texts, how modern scholarship has come to understand them, and the questions that might be raised in light of academic study. This is not in order that an Advent study might become preoccupied by such questions, but rather that they should not become an undue distraction, while at the same time enabling some exploration of the issues to become an opportunity for learning and growth.

Modern scholarship, particularly in the universities of western Europe and North America, has for the last century and more increasingly studied the biblical texts in the same way as any other ancient document.

In theory, this means that Christian beliefs and theological traditions do not influence how scholars read and interpret the texts, or relate them to what can be known of the societies and cultures in which they were written. Archaeological findings have provided alternative sources of information on life in the ancient world, but seldom furnish the evidence to corroborate specific events recorded in ancient texts.

Scholars do not agree on many aspects of the texts that will be considered in these studies. It is impossible to be certain when texts were written, or by whom, or to reconstruct whether or not events took place precisely as described. In many respects this is unimportant. Nevertheless, particularly as we prepare to celebrate Christmas, we are reminded very powerfully that our faith is rooted in historical events, in which God was perceived to be at work in the world, in quite unique ways.

There are "conservative" scholars, particularly but not only in the evangelical tradition, who believe the events told in Scripture took place essentially as recounted. Others, sometimes called "radicals" or "revisionists", sometimes "liberals", argue that the Old Testament books in particular were written centuries after the events they report, and cannot be understood as historical accounts, but rather as collections of folktales, myths, reconstructed epics—the terms used vary—and that, in the absence of archaeological evidence to confirm the stories, it should be assumed the people mentioned never lived, and the events recounted never took place. This overlooks the nature and limitations of archaeology as a science; remains that are discovered or excavated do not speak for themselves but need to be analysed and interpreted; this involves identifying and dating the artefact, interpreting any textual or other imagery, and associating it with such cultural groups and historical events as may be known from other sources. Much of this is speculative, and there remains a great deal we simply cannot know by these means. Particularly where sites have continued to be occupied to the present day, access to older layers can be difficult if not impossible, and successive programmes of building may have disturbed or reused material remains from a previous era.

No dogmatic position is taken on the historicity of particular texts; the documents are part of Christian Scripture, and the stories are important and meaningful for that reason. One particular area of sensitivity, however, should be recognized. There is a tendency among both conservative and revisionist scholars with strong convictions about Israel and Palestine to connect their findings to contemporary political issues. Many, but not all, conservative scholars see the historical events recounted and the prophecies recorded in the Old Testament as constituting and validating claims that the Zionist movement and the modern state of Israel fulfil biblical prophecies of the restoration of Israel. Modern Israel is accordingly entitled to occupy the land inhabited by ancient Israel as an exclusive Jewish state, and to expel or even to exterminate anyone else they find living there. On the other hand, some revisionists would go as far as to argue that no ancient Israel ever existed, and the Old Testament narratives are legends without any historical basis. This in itself goes beyond the evidence: the absence of archaeological corroboration does not in itself mean that events did not take place or that people never existed. Not all who hold revisionist positions are antisemites, but their writings, especially when not fully understood, can be used by antisemites. At the very least, we need to recognize that the narratives, as well as the laws and the prophetic writings, contained in the books which Christians call the Old Testament, have been formative for Jewish identity for longer than there have been Christians, and that the same traditions have subsequently contributed also to the formation of Islam.

As Christians we need to take particular care both not to give overt expression to antisemitic ideas, and also to avoid giving the impression of antisemitism. At times, this can require particular sensitivity and tact on the part of Christian leaders, particularly when biblical stories bring to mind the present experience of the Palestinian people. It is important at all times not to equate the actions of the Israeli government and its armed forces with Judaism: many Israelis are far from being observant Jews, and many Jews are vehemently opposed to the Zionist project, believe very firmly in

God's requirement of justice, and work quite selflessly for justice in the world today.

Just as it is important to be aware of Jewish sensibilities when studying biblical traditions we share, but about which we disagree quite fundamentally, so it is important that we appreciate also the significance of Jesus and his mother, Mary, and of figures from the Christian Old Testament for Muslims. Relevant passages from the Qur'an are accordingly also cited, not because these passages are in any way comparable to Christian Scripture—quite clearly they are not—but the traditions which have formed our faith have been received also by others, Muslims as well as Jews, who understand them very differently. While as Christians we remain faithful to what God has revealed to us in Christ, we recognize also that others have experienced God in different ways.

There are six studies in this book, headed Rachel, Ruth, David, Elijah, Jesus, and Epiphany Reflection. These may be used in a variety of ways. It is envisaged that the final session take place after Christmas, about Epiphany time, so that the birth of Jesus and the events surrounding it may be reflected upon again, from the perspective of God in Christ being made known to the world. The first two studies could be covered in a single session, and/or the fourth omitted (as Elijah's connections with Bethlehem are more tenuous than the others), if the fourth week of Advent does not allow for a session then. Alternatively, the course could begin during the week before Advent, to allow more time for introductory discussion and to enable a new group to cohere at the beginning of the programme. The fifth and sixth sessions might both be held about Epiphany time, reserving the first four for the season of Advent. Leaders will be able to determine which pattern is most appropriate to their particular circumstances.

Further reading

Brueggemann, Walter, *The Land: Place as Gift, Promise, and Challenge in Biblical Faith*, 2nd edn (Minneapolis, MN: Fortress, 2002).

Brueggemann, Walter, *Chosen? Reading the Bible amid the Israeli–Palestinian Conflict* (Louisville, KY: Westminster John Knox Press, 2015).

Burge, Gary M., *Whose Land? Whose Promise? What Christians are not being told about Israel and the Palestinians* (Carlisle: Paternoster, 2003).

Chapman, Colin, *Christian Zionism and the Restoration of Israel: How should we interpret the Scriptures?* (Eugene, OR: Cascade, 2021)

Dijkstra, Meindert, *Palestine and Israel: A Concealed History* (Eugene, OR: Pickwick, 2023).

Habel, Norman C., *The Land is Mine: Six Biblical Land Ideologies* (Minneapolis. MN: Fortress, 1995).

Isaac, Munther, *From Land to Lands, from Eden to the Renewed Earth: A Christ-Centred Biblical Theology of the Promised Land* (Carlisle: Langham, 2015).

Isaac, Munther, *Promised Land or Lands of Promise? Understanding Israel Today in the Light of Christ* (Oxford: Regnum, 2025).

Marchadour, Alan & David Neuhaus, *The Land, the Bible, and History: Toward the Land That I Will Show You* (New York: Fordham University Press, 2007).

Raheb, Mitri, *Faith in the Face of Empire: The Bible through Palestinian Eyes* (Maryknoll NY: Orbis, 2014).

Tarazi, Paul Nadim, *Land and Covenant* (St Paul, MN: OCABS Press, 2009).

Printed in Dunstable, United Kingdom